OVERCOMING GIANTS

*Breaking Through Barriers
Reaching Your Divine Destiny!*

RON KRAMER

Copyright © 2017 by Ron Kramer
ISBN: 978-1-940359-54-0
Library of Congress Registration: 2017954572
Published in the United States of America

All rights reserved. No part of this book may be used or reproduced by any means, graphic, electronic, or mechanical, including photocopying, recording, taping or by any information storage retrieval system without the written permission of the publisher except in the case of brief quotations embodied in critical articles and reviews.

Scripture quotations, unless otherwise noted, are taken from the NEW AMERICAN STANDARD BIBLE®, Copyright © 1960,196 2,1963,1968,1971,1972,1973,1975,1977,1995 by The Lockman Foundation. Used by permission.

Scripture quotations marked with NIV, are taken from THE HOLY BIBLE, NEW INTERNATIONAL VERSION®, NIV® Copyright © 1973, 1978, 1984, 2011 by Biblica, Inc.® Used by permission. All rights reserved worldwide.

Cover by Amanda Grace Butt

Bedford, Texas

DEDICATION

This book is dedicated to some of the most important people in my life: first, to my grandmother Marie Pitting. Her quiet, yet deep faith significantly impacted my earliest days.

This book is also dedicated to my father and mother, George and Rosemary Kramer, who sacrificed and worked tirelessly, doing all that they could with what they knew to raise me in a godly way.

I also dedicate it to my wife who has stood with me, and for me for over 32 years.

In addition, this book is dedicated to my two sons, Jesse and Jordan, who have grown to be more than my sons but also men whom I admire.

Lastly, this book is dedicated to my two grandchildren, Molly Rose and Owen Francis, as well as all those who may follow. It is my prayer that even as I have learned so much from past generations, this book will help them to walk in all the fullness of the calling of God on their lives, both now and in the future.

Keith,

I wanted to honor Ermalene in my first book because she was a real encouragement to me.

You have also been a true friend!

Ron

ACKNOWLEDGMENTS

There are a great many individuals that I could acknowledge as having a tremendous influence in my life. To name them all is not possible in this venue. Here are just a few:

Thanks to Dave Page, the first person who ever encouraged me to believe that God could work through me to teach His Word.

Then you, pastors Fred Sindorf, Skip Whitcomb, Warren Matson, Jerry Brooks, Robb Brewer, and all of the others who allowed me the opportunity to teach in youth groups, retreats, Sunday school classes and during services. They provided an opportunity for my gift to develop. I also thank Dave and Evelyn Szymanski, two people with whom I ministered with on a number of occasions. Much of the material in this book resulted from my preparation to serve with them.

A special thanks to Ermalene Czarniak; she not only encouraged me to write but spent many hours assisting me. Along with her, I want to thank Drs. Kerry and Chiqui Wood. Along with their influence through their life message of relational transformation, they both offered much encouragement and assistance with this book.

Lastly, I want to thank Dr. Carroll Thompson. His compassion for people and passion to see believers walk in the full freedom that is theirs through Christ, sparked a desire in me to express God's heart when ministering to others.

CONTENTS

Dedication
Acknowledgments
Foreword by Dr. Kerry Wood

Preface	IX
Introduction	XI

The Valley: Where the Battle Takes Place	17
The Giants We Face	25
Giants: Barriers, Bullies, and Beatable	31
David: Shepherd, King, Giant-Killer	49
David's First "Stone"—A Proper Mindset	55
David's Powerful Memory—God's Past Victories	69
David's Proven Method—A Sling and a Stone	77
David's Propelling Momentum—Words and Actions of Faith	83
David's Pure Motive—God's Glory!	97
Goliath's Sword in Our Hand—Our Testimony	103
Jesus—The Son of David Jesus—The "Giant-Killer"	111
Your Turn	117

About the Author

FOREWORD

God's stories continue to be written, mostly with unsuspecting shepherd boys, under-rated younger brothers, and sisters, delivery men carrying bread and cheese, mere teenagers, and those who have been practicing their slingshot skills on the backside of nowhere. Nobody has heard about their fight with the lion and the bear, or the naked tree that lost its bark from the thousands of practice stones. This book is your story, still being written. We call it "the story of David and Goliath," but it's more. David's story is an arch-typical story that spans across age, gender, education level, socio-economic class or religious background. It reaches into the deepest place of all of us to call out God's story—God's desire to know and be known through frail humans. Moses stuttered but had a rod. Elisha had a used mantle. David had five nothing-special stones. And you have been given something that, with a heart of faith and a word on your tongue, can bring God's awesome goodness to be seen in our day. You were uniquely made to carry the declaration of one facet of who God is, that may not be seen or known lest you pick up your mantle, your rod, your stone. Keep reading.

Ron Kramer is much like David, faithfully tending sheep, carrying bread and cheese, dutifully carrying out his Father's will, for years. I have been privileged to watch him pepper the tree with his slingshot, so to speak. I have had the joy of knowing Ron as the conscientious student working on his Master's – one of those front row guys taking meticulous notes and submitting well-researched papers. I have been blessed to serve with him pastorally in Gateway Church's Equipping Ministry—and watched him become the workhorse everyone depended upon. I know him as a loving husband, the caring father and doting grandfather, the affirming manager, and the tender worshipper. But when he wasn't tending the sheep he was working on his marksman skills. Overcoming Giants is the gift from a fellow giant slayer—written by a guy that's been peppering the tree and taking out lions and bears on the backside of nowhere. Now you get to see God's story through Ron's eyes, so as not to forget to pick up your own five smooth stones and walk into your own God-story.

Dr. Kerry Wood
Pastor, Professor, Friend,
Fellow Slingshot Fraternity Member

PREFACE

The Sunday evening service was drawing to a close. It had been a rewarding but tiring weekend, and I was ready to head home. As my pastor closed the service, I vaguely remember him previewing an upcoming message from the life of David.

Though my thoughts had already left the building, his words arrested my attention. I sensed the Holy Spirit "whispering" deep within my heart: "There are some things in life that cannot be avoided. You have to confront them and defeat them in order to get to where I'm calling you."

The message was so unexpected yet clear that I could not help but sit a moment longer and ponder what I heard inside. During my drive home, I continued to reflect on what I sensed the Lord had just spoken to my heart. Though I had been a believer for decades, I searched my heart desiring to know if there was something in my life to which the Lord was speaking. Was there something keeping me from experiencing God's best for my life?

Little did I know at the time that this moment would be the spark for motivating me to examine my own life in search for issues that may be holding me back from God's full plan for my life. Over time, I also developed a teaching on the story of David and Goliath that dealt with the need for us to confront those things that stand between us and God's best for our lives. As often as I shared it, people told me that the message helped them to recognize the need to face some issue in their life with God's help.

That unsuspecting moment at the end of a Sunday evening service and the teaching it inspired has become the contents of this book. The story of David and Goliath is a picture of the "giants" that all us face that seek to keep us from God's best. I don't claim to have all the theological answers as to why God miraculously removes some obstacles out of our path while others require a battle. What I do know is this: God can give us victory over anything that stands between us and God's best plan for our lives even as He gave David victory over Goliath.

If there seems to be something in your life that is keeping you from your God-given dream: this book is for you. If you find that your feelings of insecurity, anxiety, or fear hold you back from stepping out into God's calling on your life: this book is for you. If you are willing to trust God and face the "giant" that stands between you and God's plan for your future: read on. In Him, You can overcome giants!

INTRODUCTION

A Familiar Story

Like a curtain gradually rising to unveil the opening act of a play, the early rays of morning light illumined the countryside. It was a new day but not a new beginning. This day was no different than the past 39. It perpetuated an all too familiar and fearful reality for Israel's army. On one side of the valley stood the Philistine army, on the other, the armies of Israel. There, in the middle of the valley, stood a Philistine warrior. Though he stood alone, this solitary combatant was not the typical military opponent. He was a champion of extraordinary size and strength. There, in the valley stood a giant of a man whose name was Goliath.

Day after day, Goliath mocked and taunted the army of Israel. He challenged them to find just one soldier with the courage and confidence to fight him. Day after day, the Israelites failed to do so. Who could blame them? Certainly, there was not a commensurate opponent for one so skilled, so experienced, so armed, or one so gigantic as Goliath. Even if Israel's army had a soldier brave enough to fight Goliath, what chance would he have at victory?

Goliath's challenge had reached its fortieth day. Israel's army had failed to produce a single opponent to take on the Philistine giant. To the army of Israel, the situation appeared to be hopeless; hopeless until a young man spoke up, a young man named David.

The account of David and Goliath is quite familiar even to those with a minimal exposure to the Bible. What children's Sunday school, Vacation Bible School or Bible teaching church has not shared the story of David and Goliath at some time? Even in non-religious circles, the battle between David and Goliath is often used as an analogy to describe a "lesser" individual in any scenario facing an opponent viewed as far superior. In the world of sports, it is not unusual for an upset victory to be described as a typical "David versus Goliath" outcome.

What Giant are you facing?

The biblical account of David and Goliath is a fascinating narrative of a young man overcoming a great giant; but how does it pertain to us in our present-day life? You and I don't face giants like Goliath. Few, if any of us will ever confront a foreign army or find ourselves in a face-to-face confrontation with a larger-than-normal adversary.

Though it is quite unlikely that we will ever find ourselves in a similar situation as David, you and I do face giants. You may be thinking to yourself: "I've never faced a giant, have I?" You haven't faced a giant like Goliath, but may I ask you the following question: Is there anything that stands between you and God's best for your life? Are you facing a financial burden that you cannot imagine ever getting out from underneath? Have you been given a medical diagnosis that doesn't provide much hope?

Perhaps the giant you face is not from the present but from your past. Does your memory of past failures prevent you from believing that God still has a plan for your future? Are you still hindered from walking in what you know God has called you to do because of what people have said about you in the past?

Though different, our giants are every bit as real as the one David faced. They come in the form of thoughts, memories and triggered emotions that stand between God's perfect plan for our lives and us. Traumatic experiences along with hurtful words and lies from the Enemy serve as obstacles to faith in God and the fulfillment of His best plans and purposes. A broken home, an abusive loved one, a humiliating event at school, a discouraging business failure are just a few of the events we can experience in life that can result with a "giant" in our thoughts and hearts that have us believing a lie about God, ourselves and our future.

The nation of Israel was at a critical point. They were confronted with a military challenge that could not be ignored or avoided without a significant consequence. A valley stood between them and the Philistines. In that valley stood Goliath, and he wasn't going to back down from his challenge.

The army of Israel had to engage him. They could not go around him, over him or under him. In order to move ahead in victory, Goliath had to be confronted and defeated. Israel had chosen not to fight, but their choice wasn't solving the problem. They were no better off than they would have been had they fled or fought and lost." The only way for Israel to move forward, the only path to victory would require the army of Israel to fight and overcome their giant.

Fortunately, the story of David and Goliath does not end with the giant's challenge. It does not finish with David's declared willingness to fight. Better still, the account does not conclude with a victory of the colossal Philistine over David. What unfolds is the great triumph of David over Goliath, a resounding victory of God over Israel's enemies.

Like the account of David and Goliath, the battle against your giant does not need to end in failure. There are practical and timeless lessons to be learned from the biblical account of David and Goliath that can be applied to your own life situations. If you desire to break free from the thought-controlling, life-defeating giant that stands between you and God's plan for your life, there is a path to victory. Like David, through the grace and power of God, you can overcome giants!

Chapter One

THE VALLEY: WHERE THE BATTLE TAKES PLACE

THE PHILISTINES AND ISRAEL —SEPARATED BY A VALLEY

We'll begin our look at the enlightening confrontation between David and Goliath by setting the stage as to where the battle took place. The book of first Samuel describes the geographical location where the Philistines and the army of Israel met for battle. The author states: *"The Philistines stood on the mountain on one side while Israel stood on the mountain on the other side, with the valley between them"* (1Samuel 17:3). This passage gives us some idea of the terrain and the position of each opposing army in the account of David and Goliath. Both armies were stationed on high ground. Each was holding their position, but neither side was advancing.

Merriam Webster defines a valley as an area of low land between hills or mountains. A valley can also be described as a low period, point, or level. The first definition denotes a geographic location. The second may describe a difficult or challenging life experience. In other words, a valley may be more than a geographical space between higher elevations. It can be descriptive of a condition, emotionally or mentally, that you and I may face. It may indicate a time in our lives when we feel "stuck" or "trapped," unable to move forward into a more desirable future. A valley may describe a perspective on life; one where we are unable to see over the "mountain" in front of us and are no longer enjoying the mountaintop experience of our past. In either case, that valley is not the mountaintop.

Geographical valleys are not always undesirable places. They can be tranquil and fertile environments of abundant life and provision. Mountain snow-melts and rain flowing down from higher elevations provide essential moisture for plants and wildlife to flourish in a valley.

As pleasant as valleys can be, they can also be dangerous habitats, leaving one quite vulnerable to danger or attack. The hills and mountains surrounding a valley can limit one's visibility. In contrast, those on higher ground can easily spot and track someone who is in a valley below them.

As stated earlier, "valley" is a word often used to describe a low point in one's life. It is not unusual to hear a person describe their life in terms of a series of peaks and valleys; the peaks being those events that brought great joy and fulfillment, and the valleys as those times that were traumatic, challenging or disappointing. Those who identify themselves as believers in Jesus may refer to trying periods in their life as going through a wilderness or a valley. A person with a positive outlook may view the valleys in life as times of preparation and appreciation of mountaintop experiences. However, if one is prone toward a more negative perspective, life's valleys make it difficult to expect, anticipate or appreciate better times.

Our "Valleys:" a Place of Battle

We have already noted that a valley separated the Philistines and the army of Israel. Scripture makes that clear. What is not clearly stated is the location from which Goliath issued his challenge. One can assume, but cannot state with certainty that Goliath stood in the valley when he made his taunts. If he did, Goliath may have returned to higher ground when Israel failed to produce an opponent. What is indisputable from the scriptural account is that the battle that eventually ensued between David and Goliath took place in the valley.

Like David, you will encounter your giants in the valleys of life. It is there that you will experience your life's most defining moments. If we are going to move forward in our Christian experience, if we are going to advance from where we are to where God is calling us, we will have to choose to meet our opponent. **We will have to battle the giants in the valleys.**

Unless you're a real "fighter," you probably have a tendency to shy away from confrontation. At times, you may be willing to hold your ground. Yet, if you have a choice, you are not one to charge into battle. You prefer to avoid any skirmish, much less an all-out fight.

As believers, we are called to be peacemakers and to go "the extra mile." However, when it comes to confronting and defeating the giants in our lives, we are required to fight. Later on, our discussion will turn toward how we can battle, not in our own strength but with God's power. For now, we must come to grips with the reality that we will experience battles in the valleys of life.

What's at Stake: Slavery or Freedom

Avoiding the valleys, or refusing to fight, is not without its consequences. In order to highlight this truth, let us consider what Goliath said to Israel:

> *Choose a man for yourselves and let him come down to me. If he is able to fight with me and kill me, then **we will become your servants**; but if I prevail against him and kill him, then **you shall become our servants and serve us**.* (emphasis added).
>
> 1 Samuel 17:8-9

Goliath declared the outcome of the battle. He stated that there would be far more at stake than two people fighting and one person prevailing. What was actually at stake was the freedom or slavery of both nations.

Goliath's terms were not unique. His challenge to decide the outcome of a war between two nations by only two combatants was not a foreign one in those days. Nevertheless, the outcome of this confrontation would affect nations in the present and, potentially future generations. The result of this battle would be the freedom or slavery of an entire nation. If Goliath's experience and stature were not enough to intimidate any Israelite from battling Goliath, the impact of defeat on the entire nation of Israel was more than enough to discourage any doubter of victory.

The nation of Israel had experienced slavery at the hands of an oppressing nation in the past. The deliverance of Israel from slavery to Egypt is one of the most detailed and recounted events throughout the Bible. For over 400 years, they were in bondage to Egypt. Moses, a Hebrew who was spared from death as a baby, was raised in the ways of Egypt. Yet, his heart was toward his people. When it became known that he had killed an Egyptian who was attacking a fellow Hebrew, he fled to the wilderness.

After forty years, God called Moses back to Egypt to deliver His people from bondage. Not only did God deliver them from Egypt; He also led them into the Promised Land. Years later, in this same land, Israel again faced the possibility of slavery to a heathen nation as a result of Goliath's challenge.

OUR SLAVERY OR FREEDOM

The stakes were high in the battle between David and Goliath. Would Israel continue to dwell and possess the land God had given them by defeating what remained of the heathen nations, or would they fall back into slavery under the brutal hand of an ungodly people? The outcome of the battle in the valley would be the determining factor. It is of utmost importance for you to understand that the battle with your giant is as critical as that of David with Goliath. What is at stake is your spiritual liberty or slavery to your giant. You may not be fully aware of how significant your battle is, but it is imperative that you understand that failing to engage and defeat your giant will keep you in slavery to your giant.

Regarding this, the apostle Peter states: *"for by what a man is overcome by this he is enslaved"* (2 Peter 2:19). Peter makes this statement in the context of false teachers and their potential effect on individuals. Yet, the truth that he communicates applies to our discussion. What we allow to overcome us will enslave us. Whatever giant we fail to fight and defeat will continue its control over our lives. Fears, failures, lies, mindsets, spoken words, whatever giant that is not defeated is the giant that enslaves you and keeps you from God's best.

Your giant may be an enslaving sinful habit that snares you in its grip. Such a giant can be one of great discouragement and shame. You know what is right, and have experienced the goodness of God in your life. Yet, you just can't seem to get free from that one issue that catches you in a moment of weakness, inattentiveness or discouragement. The giant that you battle often squelches the joy of the Lord, especially in those times when you fail to stand and resist.

Facing a giant does not mean that you are in a constant, conscious state of warfare. Every moment of your life is not filled with conflict. Unlike Goliath who came forward day after day, you may be "free" of your giant most of the time. It just seems to show up when you attempt to move forward in your faith or when you are close to stepping into the call of God on your life. In other words, your giant only appears on the scene at the most critical moments!

It is then that we find ourselves in the valley of decision. Do we fight? Do we "freeze" or do we flee? If we fail to fight, we remain defeated and continue to be enslaved by our giant. Failing to engage our giant leads to the same result as fleeing. Remember, our enemy doesn't need to send us fleeing the battle in order to defeat us. As long as we are not moving forward, our giant keeps us from moving into God's perfect plan for our lives. "Fear" tells us that we are likely to go down in defeat if we battle our giant, but failing to fight or fleeing from the battle guarantees our defeat.

It is often in the valleys of life where we find ourselves face to face with that which seeks to keep us from all that God has for us. If we don't fight, we remain enslaved to the past, defeated by our giant. Yes, the battle with your giant is no insignificant matter. What's at stake is your freedom. Later, we will learn that it is not only a matter of your slavery or freedom but that of other people as well.

The valley where we face our giant can appear to be a lonely place. You may have friends and family all around you; but even as David faced Goliath in the valley, in your valley, you feel as if it's just you and your giant.

Be encouraged! You will never face your giant by yourself. God was with David when he faced Goliath, and He will be with you when you face your giant!

Chapter Two

THE GIANTS WE FACE

THE PHILISTINES: ISRAEL'S ENEMY

Valuable insight can be gained about the giant you may face by looking at one of Israel's most persistent enemies, the Philistines. The book of Judges has much to tell us in this regard. Though Joshua had successfully helped Israel defeat many of their adversaries in the Promised Land, the Philistines remained their nemesis. Shortly before his death, the Lord said to Joshua,

You are old and advanced in years, and very much of the land remains to be possessed. This is the land that remains: all the regions of the Philistines.
Joshua 13:1-2a

Though the Philistines often oppressed Israel, it is pertinent to note that it was the result of Israel's own disobedience. This is plainly stated in the book of Judges:

Now the sons of Israel again did evil in the sight of the Lord, so that the Lord gave them into the hands of the Philistines forty years.
Judges 13:1

Nevertheless, in spite of his own moral flaws, God raised up a man named Samson to deliver His people from their oppressors. In the final moments of his life, Samson pulled down a pagan temple upon himself and the Philistines. Here's what the Bible states about this event:

> *So the dead whom he killed in his death were more than those whom he killed in his life.*
>
> Judges 16:30

The battle between Israel and the Philistines continued beyond the days of the judges. Several chapters before the account of David and Goliath, we find Israel going into battle against the Philistines. Israel suffered defeat at their hands. Then, in an effort to gain an advantage over the Philistines, Israel brought the Ark of God with them into battle. The result was no different. Israel again suffered defeat. Moreover, the ark of God was captured (1 Samuel 4:11).

In time, the Philistines returned it after determining that the plague-like outbreak of tumors and infestation of rodents they experienced was a direct result of the Ark being in their possession. The Ark of God was back with Israel, but the Philistines remained their enemy.

GOLIATH'S STATURE

With this brief historical backdrop, we return to the confrontation that preceded the battle between David and Goliath. Earlier we saw how Israel had taken a position on one mountaintop, while the Philistines occupied one opposite them on the other side of a valley. Both were accustomed to skirmishes, but this scenario was different. This battle would not be between two armies but two warriors.

Out from the ranks of the Philistines emerged a man first described as a *"champion … named Goliath"* (1 Samuel 17:4). Then, we are made aware of what was likely the most distinguishing characteristic of Goliath, his height, stated to have been *"six cubits and a span"* (1 Samuel 17:4). Depending on how one calculates the length of a cubit, Goliath may have been anywhere from nine to 11 feet tall!

Goliath is not the first "giant" that is spoken of in Scripture. The 12 spies that returned from the Promised Land reported seeing giants. Here is the spies' description of their encounter with the inhabitants of the land: *"we became like grasshoppers in our own sight, and so we were in their sight"* (Numbers 13:33). Clearly, the people whom the spies had seen were significantly taller than the average person of their day.

In addition to Goliath's height, we are provided with a description of his armor and weapon that also reveals his great size. Goliath was clothed with scale armor that weighed *"five thousand shekels of bronze"* (1 Samuel 17:5). We are also told that *"the shaft of his spear was like a weaver's beam, and the head of his spear weighed six hundred shekels of iron"* (1 Samuel 17:7). These weights and descriptions may mean little to us today. After all, how many people today have any idea of how big a weaver's beam is or how much a shekel weighs? You and I may have no clue, but those who were alive in those days certainly did! There is no doubt that this description of Goliath's spear and spearhead revealed that his weapons were significantly larger and heavier than that of the average soldier.

Goliath's great stature is also attested to by the fact that no one from the army of Israel was willing to fight him. The fact that Goliath was a "champion" may not have been a sufficient reason for Israel's army not having produced an opponent to challenge him. Certainly, Israel's army must have included at least a few brave men who were experienced in fighting formidable opponents. Israel was not unfamiliar with warfare, and they had their share of battle-tested men. Yet, there was none willing to confront this giant of a man named Goliath.

Goliath's Stubbornness

For forty days, Goliath taunted Israel and challenged them to produce a challenger. For forty days, Israel failed to do so. Day after day, Goliath came forward. Day after day, no one from Israel took up his challenge.

Though Israel failed to produce a challenger, the Philistines did not change their strategy. They did not move on to "plan B." The Philistines stubbornly continued to define and enforce the terms of the battle laid down by Goliath. He had come forth, and he would have to be confronted. There was no way under, over or around this giant. The only way forward, the only way to the next mountaintop, the only way to victory was to engage and defeat Goliath.

Goliath's Speech

As if Goliath's size and stubbornness were not enough to intimidate the army of Israel, his words barraged them as well. Listen to his verbal assault:

He [Goliath] stood and shouted ... choose a man for yourselves and let him come down to me. If he is able to fight with me and kill me, then we will become your servants; but if I prevail against him and kill him, then you shall become our servants and serve us. I defy the ranks of Israel this day.

1 Samuel 17:8-10

Goliath's verbal challenge and threats must have rattled even the bravest defender of Israel. In addition to his menacing words, one can only imagine how the voice of such a giant like Goliath must have sounded: deeper than any normal man, resounding, perhaps even echoing off of the hills!

His words, like a wrangler's lasso, fell upon Israel's ears and fear's grip tightened around their hearts. Even though David had later approached him for battle in the valley, Goliath continued to hurl his verbal taunts. We will address Goliath's threats to David in the valley at a later time.

Goliath's Sentence

It is important to remember not only the terms of the battle, which Goliath set forth but also the consequence. As we have already discussed, the loser, along with his entire nation, would be subjected to a life of servitude to the victor. As risky as the battle itself would be to each combatant, the consequences of failure would have a grave impact on each other's entire nation. Clearly, this battle entailed far more than a mere determination of which army possessed the most valiant warrior. The confrontation between David and Goliath was not merely an "arm-wrestling" type of event to decide which man was stronger. At stake was an entire nation's freedom or slavery.

Just like Goliath, it may appear that the giant you face sets the terms and the consequences of the battle. Later, we will learn that if your giant has any say at all in the terms and consequences, it only does so before we defeat them! The giant you face is not in control—God is! If it appears that the enemy is setting the rules for defeat, be encouraged. Your God defines the result of victory!

Chapter Three

GIANTS: BARRIERS, BULLIES, AND BEATABLE

"Giants" are Barriers

While driving down a tranquil country road on a beautiful spring morning, "Sue" is elated. For years, she has felt a calling on her life to teach children. Opportunities for her to fulfill her dream always seemed to be out of reach, that is until today. This morning, Sue will be teaching her first Sunday school class!

With ample preparation in prayer and study; Sue, filled with the excitement of a child on Christmas morning, heads for church. As she ponders what is about to happen, tears of joy begin to cascade gently down her cheeks.

Then, like a thief, the memory of a painful experience from the fourth-grade rips the joy from her heart. Sue is now overwhelmed with fear and feelings of inferiority like she hasn't felt for some time, at least not since the last time she considered teaching children.

Reluctantly, Sue pulls into the local grocery store parking lot and calls her pastor. She leaves a voicemail, apologizing for giving him such a late notice and states that she can't teach this morning because she isn't feeling well. As she heads back home, the weights of shame and hopelessness are stacked upon the heaviness she feels in her heart from fear and inferiority. Both are the results of a painful childhood experience that continues to be the obstacle between Sue and God's call upon her life.

I present this story about Sue as an illustration of how barriers can prevent us from reaching our God-given destiny. Not every detail is based on a factual account, but it certainly isn't fiction either. Many people are hindered from moving forward in God's calling on their life by a barrier constructed from a painful experience from the past.

In life, we will face barriers. Some are intended to prohibit our spiritual progress, but others are designed to provide us protection from danger. Pushing through barriers that are designed for our protection can be devastating. Therefore, it is critical that we do not view every barrier as something that the enemy has placed in our path to hinder our progress.

Before relocating to Texas from Wisconsin, my wife and I made several exploratory visits to scout out the area in which we would be living. While driving during one of those visits, it became necessary for us to change our southern course and head east. As I approached the ramp, what I saw grabbed my attention. In front of me was something that looked less like a highway and more like the initial stage of a roller-coaster ride that takes you slowly to the highest point before hurling you down a steep descent—and I don't like rides! I could not recall a time in my life when I had traveled on an expressway that was so high off the ground.

I later learned that Texas had some of the highest overpasses in the country. The well-known "High Five Interchange" in Dallas is where Interstate 635 and US Highway 75 meet. It consists of 37 bridges with five layers of intersecting and crossing roadways; the tallest of which is 120 feet in the air (*Dallas' High Five Interchange*; Kyle Kusch, 3-22-11).

This was not the interchange on which we were traveling, but I could not imagine one being any higher off the ground than the one we were about to enter. My uneasiness was slightly relieved when I noticed concrete, guardrail barriers on both sides of the overpass. These barriers were not built to keep my wife and me from reaching our destination. They were placed there to help us reach it! Without these guardrail barriers, any type of accident would likely cause a vehicle to plunge dozens of feet onto the road below—a fall from which no one would survive.

Barriers often appear to be little more than frustrating deterrents to great excitement and adventure to many children and teenagers. However, a discerning, mature adult recognizes their value. Some barriers are a welcomed sight to anyone who recognizes their value as safeguards from the potential dangers.

Though barriers can be of great benefit, they can also prohibit spiritual progress. For example, the heathen nations in the Promised Land were not barriers of protection. They sought to prevent the progress of the nation of Israel. God's people needed to overcome these barriers in order to possess the land that God had given them.

In order to know how best to respond to any barrier we face, it is essential to possess the ability to discern the difference between a protective barrier and an obstacle that the enemy is using in an attempt to prevent us from moving forward in our spiritual life. There is potentially great danger in ignoring a barrier that is designed to protect us from harm. It is equally detrimental to fail to overcome barriers that are intended to hinder our spiritual progress. Every believer needs to be able to discern and distinguish between the barriers God has placed in our lives for our protection and ones the enemy has erected in an attempt to prevent our spiritual progress. One way to do so is by asking yourself this question: "Is this barrier in my life helping me to bear fruit or hindering me from bearing fruit?"

God has called us to bear fruit and to fulfill His purpose for our lives. However, God will prepare us for His work. At times, His preparation may actually appear to be unnecessary delays. Like Joseph, there may be times when God will allow us to go through challenging circumstances in order to prepare us for greater fruitfulness. If we are concerned that the right "doors" are not opening fast enough for us, it may be that we are not yet ready to walk in all that God has for us. In these times, we need to stay faithful, knowing that God will fulfill His promises when the time is right

However, we must never forget that the enemy will oppose us. Satan does not want us to step into God's calling on our lives. It is also possible that the enemy has placed a barrier in your path that will not be removed until you overcome it in the power of the Holy Spirit. Therefore, we must pray for God to show us if the barrier we are facing is for our protection or hindering our spiritual progress.

Goliath was not a protective barrier. He was a preventer of progress. We have discussed how Goliath stood between the armies of Israel and the Philistines for a period of forty days, preventing their advance. Israel was not able to move forward until, and unless, they defeated him. The giant they faced was determined to defy and deter Israel. As a result, Israel remained where they were.

This truth carries great significance for us as we consider the giants that we face. Whatever your giant, it is a barrier in your life that prevents you from moving forward in your Christian walk and calling. It stands between you and God's best for your life. **Your giant is a hindrance, an obstacle, that desires and acts to prevent your progress.**

Reading the story of David and Goliath, a person might miss the reality that Goliath did not need to fight and defeat anyone in order to keep the army of Israel from advancing. As long as they were unwilling to engage him, they were prevented from moving forward. This is a critical truth for us to recognize about the giants we face. Our giant does not need to advance and engage us in battle. They defeat us as long as we refuse to fight. Dealing with issues that hold us back can be challenging, difficult, painful, even frightening.

Though this is the case, they will not wander off or disappear from our lives as a result of our unwillingness to engage them in battle. Any attempt on our part to try and ignore our giant will not render them ineffective or impotent. Unless we fight, they will continue to taunt and hold their ground, keeping us from moving forward into God's best. As long as we allow the giant before us to stand unchallenged, it remains a barrier between us and God's best plans and purposes for our lives.

Every giant that we face of this nature is Satan's tool. His desire is to keep you from experiencing the freedom that is yours in Christ and the fruitfulness God desires for your life. He will do everything possible to place barriers between you and God's best. Satan's giants are not barriers to protect you from harm but to hinder your spiritual progress.

The Barriers of Painful Childhood Experiences

Satan will use painful childhood experiences, including emotional and sexual abuse, to damage your self-image. His goal is to instill a belief that you are not worthy of God's love and favor. Such mindsets and perspectives make it difficult for us to believe God has a meaningful plan for our lives. When the Holy Spirit places God's calling upon your heart, you don't have the faith to believe it. You may ask yourself, "How could God call someone as unworthy and unholy as me?" As a result, you fail to move forward into His divine plan.

It's time to return to our illustration about Sue. We'll pick up the story much earlier in her life to gain an understanding of how the barrier was built in her life. The unwelcomed buzz of an alarm clock rouses a fourth-grader from a deep sleep. With her eyes still closed, "Susie" drops her feet to the floor and makes her way to the bathroom. Her comb removes the snarls in her hair, but it has no effect on the anxiety in her heart.

It isn't long before her father notices that she is taking longer than usual to complete her morning routine. It's apparent to Susie's father that something is bothering her. When she reluctantly makes her way to the kitchen. Her father asks: "What's wrong Susie?" She replies, "I don't feel well."

Susie's father gently places his hand onto her forehead. The absence of warmth accompanied by the expression on Susie's face lets him know that it is not an illness that is affecting his daughter this morning. Removing his hand, he looks caringly into Susie's teary, hazel eyes and solicits his daughter to tell him the real problem. "I just can't go to school today daddy." Her father makes another attempt to uncover the real issue, but his daughter simply replies, "I just can't."

Yesterday was oral book report day in class. Susie was actually looking forward to telling the class about the fascinating book she read about butterflies. Susie loved the outdoors, and she recently began collecting butterflies; their wings are so pretty and colorful.

Susie, the teacher declares, "It's your turn." With a smile on her face and excitement in her heart, she clasps her book and makes her way to the front of the class. As she pans the room, her eyes fall upon the one student that always picks on her. There's no good reason for him doing so; it just seems as if he gets pleasure out of trying to make her feel uncomfortable about herself.

Susie begins her presentation and stumbles trying to pronounce a multi-syllable butterfly name. Of course, Bobby begins to laugh, quiet enough for the teacher not to hear, but loud enough for Susie's sensitive ear. With her confidence failing and her joy waning, Susie continues. While reading the next sentence, she mispronounces another word. The whole class is now chuckling. Susie is crushed under the embarrassment and begins to cry. Rather than finding compassion from her peers, her tears only make matters worse. In an effort to protect Susie from further humiliation, her teacher tells Susie that she can finish her report tomorrow.

"Tomorrow" has become "today." The last thing Susie wants to do is stand before her class again. There is no guarantee that today's experience will be any better than yesterday's. She fears it will even be worse, as hard as that is for her to imagine! Susie concludes that her only way of avoiding another painfully embarrassing moment is to stay home from school, but she's too ashamed to tell her father about what had happened. She just wants to run.

Her attempt to avoid school by faking an illness failed. Unable to get an answer as to why Susie does not want to go to school, her father tries to encourage her. He states that her day at school will be a fun time with her friends. Susie knows better.

You may ask, "How can such a typical childhood experience become a barrier that keeps a person from fulfilling God's calling?" The enemy uses these experiences to form lies about one's view of God as well as one's own identity. Painful childhood experiences are bricks that Satan forms into walls that discourage a person from moving into their calling. The call of God may be clear, but we become convinced that the giant that stands between us and it cannot be overcome.

Let's continue the story. As an adult, Sue hears about a need for a Sunday school teacher in the children's department at her church. As the pastor expresses his desire for a new volunteer, Sue senses the Holy Spirit stirring her heart. For years, she has had a desire to teach children. After expressing her passion, Sue's pastor encourages her to teach next week.

Today, Sue will be teaching her first children's Sunday school class. As she drives to church, the memory of her painful fourth-grade experience suddenly engulfs her thoughts. It was so long ago, but she feels as if her embarrassing moment happened this morning. "You can't speak in front of people," whispers the discouraging voice that she has heard since that traumatic day in the fourth-grade. As an adult, Sue uses the same excuse that she did as a child. She tells her pastor that she isn't feeling well. As an adult, there is no father present to invalidate her story. Her pastor says that he understands and quickly finds a replacement teacher. Sue is prevented from stepping into her divine calling by a barrier that is built on her past.

The painful childhood experiences of sexual and physical abuse often inflict much greater emotional wounds than what Susie experienced in our illustration. Yet, experiences that may appear to be far less life altering than stumbling through a book report can become the material from which Satan constructs barriers. Such barriers prevent us from moving forward into God's best plans and purposes for our lives.

May I ask you: What childhood experiences have become barriers in your life? Did you finish last in a competition to your father's expressed displeasure? How embarrassed were you when the girl you had a crush on in high school laughingly rejected your offer for a date in front of your classmates? Was there someone in your life around whom you should have felt safe that abused you? You may have "convinced" yourself that your experience wasn't so bad. You may think that you are over it. After all, it happened years ago. You've grown up. However, if there is a memory or experience that comes to mind every time you attempt to move beyond where you are to where you believe God is calling you, there may well be a giant in your life that needs to be confronted and defeated.

GIANTS ARE BULLIES

There is a great deal of conversation today about bullying. It is a serious problem in many schools. A forty-year study of bullying was conducted. Some of the findings of that study are stated in the May-June 2015 article of the *American Psychologist*. Research indicates that as many as 33% of all students have been the victims of bullying. A significant number of these students were consistently bullied between the ages of 8 and 16. The percentage of students from the 4th to the 12th grade who have experienced physical bullying may be as high as 31%. Not only do many students find themselves being bullied physically, others are also bullied by verbal taunts and threats. Fortunately, the study seemed to confirm that traditional forms of bullying are declining. However, with the ever-increasing access to technology, it appears that cyberbullying is on the rise.

Every school that I ever attended had a bully. Oftentimes, it was the biggest boy who used his size to intimidate others. Bullying was not exclusive to males. Girls who were attractive and popular would rally others to mercilessly pick on someone with a complexion issue, another who wore glasses, or one whose parents could not afford the latest style of clothing.

Painful events in a child's life may lead them to bully others. Bullies, themselves, may have been targets of bullying by older siblings in their homes. Others may have been the victims of physical abuse. As a result, they bullied others to reverse their experience at home.

Whatever the reason, those who were bullied cared little about what motivated those who bullied them; they were too busy trying to protect themselves. Though some bullies were quite mean; others were more of a pest than a physical threat. In either case, they were no fun to be around, especially if you were the one being bullied.

In elementary school, I was always one of the smallest kids in my class. At my school, there was a group of guys that were part of the "in-crowd." If you figured that I wasn't a part of that group, your assumption would be correct. For the most part, that bunch of boys wasn't overly mean to those outside their circle, but the potential was there. Not only were they some of the most popular guys in the school, they were also some of the biggest and strongest ones.

There was one exception. We'll call him John. He was clearly the smallest of the bunch. In fact, he was close to my size. Nevertheless, I was afraid of him.

There was a time when, on a daily basis, John would pick on me at the beginning of each recess period. As I look back, I think he did so to prove that he belonged in the "in-crowd." There was only one boy in school that was smaller than me, so I was a perfect target.

After lunch was over, John would track me down and initiate an unsolicited wrestling match that always ended with him pinning me to the ground. Once he did so, the contest was over, and he left me alone for the rest of the day.

I was never really that frightened of John. What scared me was his circle of friends. They always encircled us as we fought. My fear was that others might join in the fight, especially if John ever got in trouble. For this reason, I never responded with any resistance to his assaults. For months, I learned to live with the unpleasant situation, believing it would never get better and fearful it could get much worse. I will save the ending to this story for later in our discussion. It will serve as an illustration as to how we can have victory over our giants.

Bullied by Hurtful Words

We have heard the words that Goliath shouted to the army of Israel. He was no "gentle giant." Goliath's words were harsh and condescending. His threats were intimidating and enslaving. It might be said that Goliath used his height, his weight, and his words to bully Israel into submission. When it comes to being a bully, our giants are no different than Goliath.

Let me share another story that may sound all too similar to you. "Jimmy" always liked playing sports. He wasn't the fastest or the strongest of his friends, but he gave his best effort every time he played.

During his early years, Jimmy was always one of the shortest and skinniest of all the kids. He was what they called a "late-bloomer." Even during his high school years, Jimmy was noticeably less mature and developed than his peers.

Gym class always ended with a painful experience for Jimmy. Everyone had to shower after it was over. Jimmy loved sports, but he hated showers—not all showers, just those that he had to take in front of the other guys. It was bad enough that Jimmy's gym shorts revealed his unusually skinny legs. The showers were far worse. There, his "failure" to have reached puberty by the time nearly ever other classmate had could not be hidden.

Name-calling is a common practice among kids. Jimmy wasn't overweight. He was quite thin. Being overweight was often a magnet for harmful words, but being skinny did not exempt Jimmy from them. His height, his weight and his later-in-life experience of physical maturity led to labels like "Stickman," "Slim Jim" and others that carried far more derogatory descriptions. Being short and skinny led Jimmy to feel inferior before both the guys and the girls in his class. Eventually, Jimmy went through his growth spurt, but the hurt continued on from the names he was called. The years of name-calling had worked their way into Jim's heart.

As an adult, others never viewed Jim to be an assertive, "take-charge" type of person. Aggression may not be a virtue, but shyness and timidity are not always desirable traits. Jim was called to be a leader, but he rarely, if ever led. Some viewed his reserved personality as humility. However, the reality was that Jim's past experiences had become a barrier to his call to lead.

Jim was wise, thoughtful and visionary, but he struggled to step into any leadership positions. He was quick to assume supportive roles, not always because of his servant's heart but often due to his feelings of inferiority. Some people didn't understand why Jim never seemed to reach his full potential in his endeavors. He seemed to have everything it would take to be successful, everything except a reasonable self-confidence and assurance that God had called him to lead others. Jim never seemed to be able to shake the personal opinion he had of himself due to the labels that were placed upon him by others. The call of God on his life was evident to those who knew him. Yet, there was a barrier that always seemed to keep him from reaching his full potential.

Jimmy is not the real name of the person I just described. His real name is Ron. The story is what I experienced while growing up. It depicts one of my personal giants that I have had to battle. Nearly everyone has to face a giant.

Words spoken to you can be some of the biggest barriers to overcome. They can penetrate one's heart and become mindsets that are difficult to dislodge. The old saying: "Sticks and stones may break my bones, but names [words] will never hurt me," sounds like a good comeback to those who "name-call," but it fails to describe reality. Words may not be able to break your bones, but they can crush your spirit. When what you've heard is a lie, the *"father of lies"* is often involved, seeking to build a barrier to keep you from moving forward spiritually.

Battle Options: Flee, "Freeze," or Fight

When Goliath stepped forward to challenge Israel's army, they were confronted with three choices: flee, freeze, or fight. All three options had the potential of ending up badly for Israel. Two of them would result in certain defeat. Only one choice could lead to victory.

Israel could have chosen to flee in the face of such an opposing enemy as Goliath. He was a champion, and he was a giant. Even if there had been one who was willing to engage him in battle, what chance would he have at victory? Fleeing may have allowed them to avoid being killed by the Philistines at that moment, but they would concede defeat by doing so.

Day after day, Goliath taunted the army of Israel. Day after day, they remained on their side of the valley. Israel didn't flee, but neither did Goliath. The Philistine did not force them to retreat, but the absence of confrontation did not allow them to advance. Holding their position may have appeared to be better than fleeing and safer than fighting, but it did not lead to victory. Israel was frozen in their position, not choosing to flee but unwilling to fight.

The only other choice was to fight. They had the option of engaging Goliath in battle, but none was willing to do so. Even though fleeing and freezing would only result in defeat, there was no guarantee that fighting would lead to a better outcome. The thought of confronting Goliath was no more pleasant than fleeing or freezing.

OUR OPTIONS IN OUR BATTLE

Regarding the giants that we face, we have the same three options available to us as did the army of Israel. We can either flee the battle scene, freeze in fear and uncertainty, or we can choose to fight. Like Israel, only one of the three options will ever allow us to overcome the giants we face.

Fleeing from our giants will not bring us victory. If we continually run from the battle, we will never move past that issue in life that holds us back. It may be a painful memory. It may be a mindset that has us convinced that things cannot change. It may be a lie of the enemy that fills us with fear every time we attempt to get past our struggle.

Fleeing may make us feel safer, more peaceful or less fearful. However, those feelings will not last. As difficult as it may seem to confront our giant, running from it will not bring about our freedom. We will remain its servant.

You may be at a point in life where you are not running from your giant, but you are also not confronting it. You have learned to live with it. You've decided that fleeing is not a desired response, but fighting simply presents too great of a risk. So, you've chosen just to live "at peace" with your giant. You've decided, "You won't bother him if he doesn't bother you." Rather than moving forward past your giant, you've decided just to be content with where you are. You'll simply live your life on this side of the valley, doing the best you can and hoping that God understands.

Trying to live at peace with your giant is no better than fleeing. Remember, Satan's goal is to use your giant to keep you from God's best, God's plan and purpose for your life. Satan does not need for you to flee in order to accomplish his goal. He just needs to keep you from moving forward. Whether you are fleeing from the battle or frozen in your position, your giant is winning. You may believe that failing to fight is more spiritual than fleeing and more peaceful than fighting. However, you are missing out on all that God desires for you, and you will never find true peace or fulfillment knowing you are not walking in His best for your life.

Giants Are "Beatable"

Goliath stood between Israel and the Philistines. He challenged Israel to a fight of which he was certain he would be victorious. He shouted at Israel. He taunted Israel. He intimidated Israel. He was a bully, both physically and verbally. As a result, he was a barrier to their progress.

Your giants are no different. They stand between you and God's plans and purpose for your life. Like Goliath, your bullies shout at you; they taunt you, and they intimidate you. Your giants are barriers to your progress as they bully you around. Like Goliath, you may think that they cannot be defeated. After all, they've held you in check for all these years. You've experienced the pain, the frustration and the oppression of your giant. There is no joy in knowing that your giant holds you back. Yet, they are terrifying to you, and you are afraid to confront them, much less, fight them.

You hoped that one day they would just go away, but they haven't. They don't always bother you, just when you try to believe the truth about yourself as revealed in God's Word. They always seem to show up just when you try to step out and do what God has called you to do. In other words, they only appear on the scene when you try to move forward in your calling.

Yes, your giant is both a barrier and a bully. Yet, there is one more thing that you must know about your giant. Your giant is beatable! **No matter how big your giant is, no matter how much of a barrier, no matter how much of a bully, your giant can be beaten!** It is now time to turn our attention away from giants and toward a young man named David. He will show us how to overcome giants.

Chapter Four

DAVID: SHEPHERD, KING, GIANT-KILLER

"Are these all the children?" This is the question that the prophet Samuel asked after Jesse had all of his sons, except for his youngest, pass before him (1Samuel 16:11). In response to the prophet's question, Jesse said, *"There remains yet the youngest, and behold, he is tending the sheep."* Without hesitation, Samuel said, *"Send and bring him; for we will not sit down until he comes here"* (1 Samuel 16:11).

Saul failed to obey the Lord's command. As a result, God called the prophet Samuel to anoint a new king. In obedience to the Lord, Samuel went to the house of Jesse to anoint God's chosen leader of His people. Seven of Jesse's sons passed before Samuel. None of them were God's choice, not even Eliab, the oldest and the tallest, the one whom most resembled Saul.

Then Samuel asked if there was yet another son. Jesse stated that there was one more, one that he apparently did not even bother to bring before the prophet. He was his youngest who was out tending the sheep. When Samuel saw him, he declared that David was the one whom God had chosen. In the eyes of his family, David was the least likely of all to have been chosen to be king.

David was the youngest. He was nothing more than a youthful shepherd. Yet, God saw something in this shepherd boy that caught His attention. Should we be surprised at God's decision to choose a shepherd to be king? After all, the One who called Himself the Good Shepherd stated that anyone who had seen Him had seen the Father. In light of this, why would anyone be surprised that God, the Supreme Shepherd, picked a shepherd to care for His people?

The Battle on Our Way to God's Calling

Early in his life, David would also have to face and defeat a giant. Though this was the case, the giant that David faced did not hinder his calling. In fact, his confrontation with Goliath actually helped to bring about its fulfillment! But this was only the case because David was willing to battle and overcome the giant that stood in the way. This may surprise you, but **even anointed kings may need to overcome giants in order to experience their calling.**

Before we look at how David defeated Goliath and what we can learn from his victory, let us take a moment to reflect on what David's "giant" experience tells us about our personal calling from the Lord. David did not simply decide, one day, to become king of Israel. He was called of God. Yet, David's actions played a part in bringing God's calling to pass. It is not the purpose of this book to examine everything that took place between David's anointing to be king and the fulfillment of that anointing. We will mainly focus upon his battle against Goliath and how that battle speaks to us today.

One may argue that David could have become king without ever having defeated Goliath. Perhaps that is true. What cannot be argued is that David's victory over Goliath had no impact on him becoming king. David's victory over Goliath played a key role in the entire process.

David's victory not only built his faith in God, it helped to build Israel's faith in David. David's victory also grabbed the attention of the Philistines, one of Israel's greatest enemies. It also did not escape the attention of Israel's first king, Saul. Perhaps most importantly, David's willingness, coupled with his motivation for wanting to battle Goliath validated God's description of him as a man after His own heart.

David faced a battle with a giant before he ever became king. So what does that have to do with you and me? Every one of us will face obstacles on the road to the fulfillment of God's purpose and calling for our lives. For you, it may entail your past. Perhaps you were not raised in a Christian home. Your history may be filled with moral failure and personal pain. You may view yourself to be one of the most unlikely of candidates for God's service. Others may have voiced a similar opinion. **Giants from the past confront us in the present, seeking to hinder us from moving forward into God's ordained future.**

Perhaps you are one who does not battle with past issues. Your giants may be present feelings of fear, insecurity, uncertainty or inferiority. Your feelings may not be based on some traumatic event from the past. They just may happen to be the type of attack that the enemy brings against you in an attempt to discourage you from moving forward. Your giant may be any one of a multitude of mental, emotional or spiritual issues that keep you from believing that you could ever battle past them into a victorious life.

Whatever giant you face, God is the One who called you, and you can be confident that He is able to bring about victory over any giant that stands between you and His plans for your life. Though this is the case, we will likely be required to engage in battles in order to experience

His victory and see His plans come to pass. Let us now look at how David defeated Goliath in order to learn how we, too, can overcome the giants we face.

David's Keys to Victory:
FIVE SMOOTH STONES

Before we pick up the story of David and Goliath from where we left off, we will, first, briefly consider David's chosen weapons for battle as a starting point. The Scripture tells us that David *"took his stick in his hand and chose for himself five smooth stones from the brook, and put them in the shepherd's bag which he had, even in his pouch, and his sling was in his hand"* (1 Samuel 17:40). At a later point, we will address why David chose the weapons that he did. For now, we will only concern ourselves with the number of stones he took from the brook.

From the river, David picked out five smooth stones to take into battle against Goliath. Some have pondered whether there is a spiritual significance to the number of stones that David took with him. Some see the number as a prophetic picture of other giants that would be defeated by David's men in the future. You can find the account of these giants and the battles against them in 2 Samuel 25. This chapter records giants named Ishbibenob, Saph, Goliath the Gittite and another who is only referred to as *"a man of great stature."* All four giants were defeated at the hands of David's men. In this portion of Scripture, we also learn that *"These four were born to the giant in Gath"* who was most likely the giant named, Goliath, which David faced and defeated (2 Samuel 21:18-22). One may view

David's five stones as a foreshadowing of victory over these five giants.

Another potential significance to the number of stones that David took may be found in the number of the original lords and major cities of the Philistines. The book of Joshua describes five lords of the Philistine territory in the Promised Land: *"the Gazite, the Ashdodite, the Ashkelonite, the Gittite and the Ekronite"* (Joshua 13:3). In the book of 1 Samuel, we find a reference to five major cities: *"Ashdod...Gaza, Ashkelon, Gath...Ekron"* (1 Samuel 6:17). It is possible that, even though David only used one stone to defeat Goliath, each of the five stones in David's pouch represented the victory over all of the lords and cities of the Philistines that David accomplished when he defeated Goliath.

There may be no way to verify these interpretations. It is possible that David simply picked up the number of stones that he knew would best fit in his sling. If he could fit five of them in his pouch, he knew he had the right ones.

David may have used only one of the five stones to defeat Goliath, but he did demonstrate five heart attitudes, or truths, in his victory over his giant. I describe these truths as David's:

1) Proper Mindset
2) Powerful Memory
3) Proven Method
4) Propelling Momentum
5) Pure Motive

Each of these played a crucial role in David's victory over Goliath. We will now explore how these truths are keys to overcoming our giants as well.

Chapter Five

DAVID'S FIRST "STONE" —A PROPER MINDSET

Earlier, we saw that one of the first things Scripture reveals about Goliath is his gigantic stature. He was over nine feet tall! The size and weight of his armor gives further evidence to his massive physique. Add to Goliath's size his verbal assault and taunt, and it is no wonder that Saul and the army of Israel *"were dismayed and greatly afraid"* (1 Samuel 17:11).

The giant you face may be no less frightening in your eyes than Goliath was to the Israelites. Fear, painful experiences, emotional trauma, insecurities, whatever giant you face may appear to be a towering, menacing giant. You may doubt whether you could ever overcome such an obstacle to your spiritual progress.

David found himself at the battlefront because his father had sent him with supplies for his brothers and their military commander. He was to bring back to his father, Jesse, a report about their condition. While he was conversing with them, Goliath came forth and spoke his usual taunts in David's hearing.

The men of Israel asked David, *"Have you seen this man who is coming up?"* (1 Samuel 17:25). Certainly, David saw what others saw when he looked at Goliath. However, David also saw what no one else seemed to notice. Goliath's great height and size captivated the eyes of Israel; yet, David looked beyond both of these physical features.

The biblical account of David's description of Goliath

has nothing to do with the giant's height, size or skill. When David asked about Goliath, he said:

Who is this uncircumcised Philistine, that he should taunt the armies of the living God?

1 Samuel 17:26

This question of David reveals the first key to David's victory over Goliath. David viewed the giant with a proper mindset.

It was not that David was unaware of Goliath's stature, armor, or weaponry. David wasn't blind to what others saw when he gazed at Goliath. It's just that **David's focus was not on Goliath's physical features but upon his spiritual condition**. This is evident by his description of Goliath as an *"uncircumcised Philistine."* Though it may be argued that Goliath was not actually a Philistine, (*The International Bible Encyclopaedia* (sic), Volume II by Wm. B. Eerdmans Publishing Company, Grand Rapids, Michigan, 1939, 1956, 1984, p. 1276), he certainly did not belong to the nation of Israel. In addition, there's no doubt as to who he was siding with in this confrontation. Therefore, David's description of Goliath is fitting. We will consider the implications and significance of both words that David used to describe Goliath.

Goliath—Uncircumcised

The first word David used to describe Goliath was the adjective, "uncircumcised." Without going into unnecessary detail, anyone familiar with circumcision is aware that the act involves the removing of a portion of skin from a male's body. At first glance, one may view David's description of Goliath as being nothing more than a physical description. After all, circumcision is a physical action that affects a male's body. Yet, David's description of Goliath had nothing to do with the giant's physical body but everything about his spiritual condition. To gain an understanding of the spiritual significance of David's description of Goliath, we will look at what the Scripture unfolds regarding the origin of circumcision.

Circumcision – A Sign of God's Covenant

In Genesis, we read of God's calling of a man named Abram. Though he would become the father of the Jewish nation, at the time of his calling, Abram is described as a Chaldean. God said to him:

Go forth from your country, and from your relatives and your father's house, to the land which I will show you; and I will make you a great nation.
Genesis 12:1-2

God was beginning His plan to establish His people.

In Genesis 17, we read of God's covenant with Abraham to make him, not just the father of the Jewish people, but also the father of a multitude of nations. God gave Abraham a sign of this covenant:

... you shall keep my covenant, you and your descendants after you throughout their generations. This is My covenant which you shall keep ... every

male among you shall be circumcised.

Genesis 17:10

The circumcision of Abraham and his descendants was to be the physical sign of the spiritual covenant between them and God. Much more could be said about the matter of circumcision. For our purposes, we will only address it as a physical sign of the exclusive covenant between God and His chosen people.

It is likely that every member of the army of Israel was circumcised. King Saul was circumcised. David's brothers were circumcised. David himself was circumcised.

All Jewish males were to be circumcised. However, the giant in the valley was not! When David described Goliath as being uncircumcised, he was referring to a condition that went beyond what could be observed physically. David's description indicated that he knew Goliath was not under the protection and provision of the covenant of God that all of Israel enjoyed.

In this way, David had a proper mindset toward Goliath. He saw beyond his physical appearance to Goliath's spiritual condition. In light of this spiritual reality, Goliath's experience and mammoth size did not intimidate David. His physical size and military skill meant nothing in light of the fact that he was uncircumcised. For David, the "bottom line" was that Goliath was not a participant in the covenant relationship that David was privileged to have with His God.

GOLIATH—A PHILISTINE

We have spoken briefly about the Philistines as Israel's

persistent enemy during the early years of their history. We will look at another aspect of these people as we discuss the significance of David's description of Goliath. Doing so will provide more insight as to how we can defeat the giants that we face.

God's covenant with Abraham included land. God's promise to him not only involved a special relationship, it also included real estate. The Lord said to Abraham, "I am the Lord who brought you out of Ur of the Chaldeans, to give you this land to possess it" (Genesis 15:7).

After Israel's deliverance from Egypt and their journey in the Wilderness, God led them to the land He had promised to His people. After the death of Moses, Joshua was the man called by God to lead his people into the land to possess it. God gave Joshua success against many of the nations that inhabited the Promised Land. However, Israel was unsuccessful at driving out all of the heathen nations.

The Philistines were one of those nations that remained. Toward the end of Joshua's life, the Lord said to him:

You are old and advanced in years, and very much of the land remains to be possessed. This is the land that remains: all the regions of the Philistines ....
Joshua 13:3

The Philistines were not the only enemies of Israel during the days of Joshua but they were a problematic foe that continued to attack and oppress Israel over the years.

It is important to note that at least some of the land that the Philistines occupied was part of the land that God had given to Israel. Therefore, they were holding on to territory that God said belonged to His people. Interestingly, the Philistines are said to have inhabited the land the Bible calls "Philistia." The Hebrew word for this region literally means "migrant," an indication that the Philistines migrated there from another country (*The International Bible Encyclopaedia, Vol. 4, James,* Orr, Eerdman's Publishing Company, 1984). A migrant is one who moves about from place to place, working, and perhaps, even living in an area that does not belong to them. After God had promised the land to Israel, the Philistines no longer had the right to inhabit it, much less possess it. Though this was the case, Israel's failure to drive them out prevented them from settling in all the territory given to them by God.

THE PROPER MINDSET TOWARD YOUR GIANT

What does this scenario of the Philistines in the Promised Land tell us about our giants? It tells us that **the giants that oppose us do not have the right to do so. Whatever "ground" they possess in our lives is not rightfully theirs to possess.** On the cross and by His resurrection, Jesus has defeated every demonic power, every giant you and I face. In his letter to the Colossians, when speaking of Christ's victory over the powers of darkness, Paul states:

> *He* [Christ] *had disarmed the rulers and authorities,*
> *He made a public display of them, having triumphed over them.*
>
> Colossians 2:15

If that is the case, why do we still face such giants as fear, insecurity, and doubt? In many cases, it is simply because we have failed to fight and overcome them. God has given us the victory, but we have not gone into battle to defeat the giants in our lives. It is true that, at times, God will miraculously remove obstacles to our spiritual growth simply by His grace. Though this may be the experience of some individuals and in some situations, like the children of Israel in the Promised Land, we are often required to take action against these giants to drive them out of where they don't belong.

When David called Goliath an uncircumcised Philistine, he was declaring that he was not a part of God's covenant people. As an uncircumcised Philistine, he was not the recipient of God's covenantal promises. He did not possess the outward sign of God's covenant that He made with Abraham and His people. Therefore, Goliath did not have the covenantal blessings of God, nor did his people have the right to the Land that was promised to Israel.

It is significant to recognize what the Bible tells us about the place where the Philistines were at the time of this confrontation. The account of David and Goliath begins like this:

> *"Now the Philistines gathered their armies for battle; and they were gathered at Socoh, **which belongs to Judah**, and they camped between Socoh and Azekah, in Ephes-dammim.*
>
> 1 Samuel 17:1

Notice that the city of Socoh did not belong to the Philistines; it belonged to the tribe of Judah! The book of Joshua states that this city was given to that tribe after they had begun to take possession of the Promised Land (Joshua 15:21, 35).

At the very beginning of this story, we come face to face with a valuable truth about our giants; they seek to possess what belongs to us. Their goal is to keep us from experiencing all that God has for us. Getting what God has given us may require a battle against a giant, but God will help us to gain what He has given to us.

When David saw Goliath, it was not his height, his size or his skill that caught his attention. David was neither fearful of, nor impressed with Goliath's physical appearance or reputation as a champion warrior. David's perspective of Goliath was not born out of any arrogance, foolishness or youthful miscalculation on his part. David simply viewed his opponent with a proper mindset. He assessed Goliath from a spiritual perspective, not a physical one.

A Proper Mindset Regarding Your Identity

A proper mindset regarding your giant is critical, but so is a proper mindset regarding our own identity. You will likely never become a giant killer if you continue to let others or your giant define you. As critical as it is to see the giant we face in light of who God is, it is also crucial that we see ourselves in the light of how God sees us. An identity based on the opinion of others or the lies of the enemy will likely hinder us from even considering that we could be victorious over our giant.

Later in this book, I will share some things about my early life that helped to establish one of the giants that I faced. For now, I will just say that there were things about my physical appearance that led me to feel that I was on the "outside" trying to find my way in. In a number of ways, my physical characteristics led me to believe that I was not like most others. This caused me to search for a way to be accepted, to find significance, to be noticed for something valuable rather than for my perceived inferiority.

During my early life, my musical gift became that which defined me. At the age of five, I demonstrated a natural ability or gifting, to play the drums. My parents were encouraged not to give me music lessons until I was seven. Once lessons began, it wasn't long before I became quite good at drumming. By the time I reached my early teens, it had become evident to all that I was clearly gifted in this area.

At a time in my life when I was much shorter, skinnier and less mature physically than my peers, my identity became tied to my musical talent. By my later teen years, it was the defining factor of my identity. It allowed me to hide behind my gift, and enabled me to avoid having to let anybody "inside." My outward talent was self-validating and provided a favorable impression of me to others.

The problem was that my identity was not based on an intrinsic value of being created by a loving God who loved me for who I was, not for how I could perform. This led to a dangerous combination of pride and insecurity. When I felt that my musical ability was superior to others, the result was not acceptance but pride. Whenever I heard another drummer who was as good or better than I was (which was always devastating to admit), my identity and self-worth came crashing down. Such a fragile shell of an identity, whether reinforced or challenged, left a gaping void inside of me.

Insecurity often leads a person to look for something to add to the "outside" to hide the void inside. It may be a fancy sports car, expensive clothes or jewelry, a house in an exclusive suburb, multiple boyfriends or a trophy wife. It can also prompt a person to make poor decisions and life choices in an effort to feel secure.

Insecure individuals create a false identity that they believe to be more acceptable or impressive to others. It is also a desperate attempt to draw their own attention away from the painful void that they know exists inside their heart. Any insecurity within may prevent you from facing the giant that is before you. In fact, a false, or deceptive view of yourself may actually be your giant! Giants that attack your identity enslave you and hold you back from God's best for your life.

A healthy identity is not one based on self-confidence, "positive thinking" or any level of arrogance or pride. It is seeing yourself as God sees you. In spite of your faults, shortcomings and past failures, God has declared that those who have placed their faith in Him are His children. God is your loving Father. As the apostle, John states: "See how great a love the Father has bestowed on us, that we would be called the children of God; and such we are" (1 John 3:1).

A proper mindset regarding your own self-image will break you free from the lies and deception of the enemy. Ask God to reveal to you any source of false identity. It can come in two forms: a false source for finding value or self-worth or a lie that causes you to believe that you are not valuable or loved by God.

This may require you to "open yourself up" to the work of the Holy Spirit. You will need to be honest with yourself and with God. You will need to come out from whatever you are hiding behind in front of others as well as God. The truth is that nothing is hidden from Him. The Lord knows all about you. The good news is that He loves you even though He knows you.

Many years ago, I spent a few days in prayer and fasting. I was desperate for an answer to a situation in my life. After several days of waiting on the Lord, I still was searching to hear from Him what I thought I needed to hear.

On the afternoon of my third day of prayer and fasting, I began to cry out to God. To my surprise, I found myself confessing a level of pride in my life that I never knew existed. Some of my pride was passed down from the influence of a previous generation. However, much of it resulted from my own self-evaluation.

After a time of confession and repentance, I felt an unexpected peace. I also had a sense that God was right next to me in the room. Then, I remember having said out loud, "You're still here!" I said it over and over again. I was sure that God wouldn't want to be near me once He found out what I was really like inside. The presence of pride in my heart was a revelation to me but not to God.

That was the beginning of a healing process of replacing an identity based on performance with one based on His unconditional love for me. God revealed my pride to break me but not to crush me. He knew that I needed to see myself for who I was apart from Him and to see His love for me in spite of my pride. The revelation of His love had a profound effect on my identity as well as my pride. The pride in my heart needed to go, but the way He did it surprised me. I can't say that I have never had to deal with pride in my heart since that time, but I can say that God brought about a lasting change in my life that afternoon.

Victory over your giant will not result simply from an understanding of your true identity. However, it is the place from where you can gain a proper perspective of your giant and an awareness of the greatness of your God. Breaking free from a false identity will enable you to view your giant and your God with a proper mindset.

Our God is greater than any giant you may face, and as your loving Father, God will fight for you. This foundation of truth, along with a proper mindset about every giant you face, will move you closer toward victory.

When others looked at David, they saw only a young shepherd, not a soldier, not a warrior, not an anointed king nor a giant killer. It is true that David was a shepherd, but he was more than that. David was also one of God's chosen people.

The source of David's faith was not his own identity. It rested in His God. However, when he described Goliath as an uncircumcised Philistine, it is clear that he saw himself as a circumcised Israelite! Therefore, he knew that His God would be with him when he faced his giant.

The same is true for us. We are not to find faith for victory over our giant from our own spiritually healthy self-image. However, when we see ourselves as God sees us, we will believe that even as God was with David, he will be with us when we face our giant. We will possess a proper mindset regarding our giant, God, and ourselves that will enable us to overcome our giant.

God Is Bigger!

How do you see your giant? Do you view your giant as David viewed Goliath or is your perspective of your giant more like that of the army of Israel? Are you focused on how big your obstacle appears to be? Are you alarmed and frightened by your giant's taunts; or are you ready for battle, overflowing with confidence that you will defeat it? It all depends on whether you are seeing your giants from a spiritual or merely a natural perspective.

Please do not feel that I am making light of any struggle you may be facing. Everyone has battled something in his or her life that was difficult to overcome. My battle may not be yours, and your battle may not be exactly like someone else's. What may seem to be an easy issue to overcome by some is extremely difficult for others. When speaking of a proper mindset, it is not my intent to make anyone feel condemned for viewing his or her giant as an insurmountable obstacle. We all have faced challenges in our lives that, at least for a time, seemed to be improbable if not impossible to overcome.

The value of this first key is simply this: **when we come to the place where we realize that no matter how big our giant appears, it is nothing compared to our great God, we are on our way to victory!** When he beheld Goliath, David did not compare his size to that of Goliath's. He did not compare his armor, his weapons or even his experience to that of Goliath. When David looked at Goliath, he compared him to His great God, and there was no comparison between the two!

Like David, when we face our giants, we must not compare them to ourselves, or we may never find the faith to believe they can be defeated. Whatever natural form our giants may take on, whether it be a broken relationship, an abusive person or emotionally crippling words that were spoken by a "friend;" the truth is, our giants are spiritual attacks from Satan. He desires to rule over us in fear. If we focus on our giant, we will likely flee. If we focus on ourselves, we will likely freeze. If we focus on God, we will begin to see our giants with a proper mindset. We will see them from a spiritual perspective. Once we do, our faith will grow, and our giant will shrink in comparison to our great God. We will then be ready to fight!

Chapter Six

DAVID'S POWERFUL MEMORY—GOD'S PAST VICTORIES

David was willing to take on Goliath because he had a proper mindset toward the giant he faced. He viewed Goliath from a spiritual perspective. David's proper mindset was only one of the five "stones" that he took into battle. We will now look at the second one; it was his powerful memory. David's vivid memory of past victories that God had helped him to achieve provided him a firm foundation of faith to believe he could defeat Goliath.

When he arrived at the battlefront, David's initial curiosity and comments about Goliath provoked a less than favorable response from his older brother Eliab. That's putting it mildly. The Scripture states that Eliab's heart *"burned with anger"* (1 Samuel 17:28). He accusingly said to David:

> *Why have you come down here? And with whom did you leave those few sheep in the desert? I know how conceited you are and how wicked your heart is ...*
> 1 Samuel 17:28, NIV

Eliab had been passed over by the prophet Samuel. When the prophet asked if he had another son, Jesse called David in from tending the sheep. David was then anointed as king. Once again, Jesse called David away from tending sheep. This time, it was for the purpose of checking on his brothers. When David arrived at the battlefront, Eliab, who was not chosen as king now stood before David as one unwilling to fight Goliath. Would David's presence again lead to an embarrassing moment for Eliab? We may not be able to determine all of the issues that played into Eliab's harsh response toward David. What is clear is that Eliab had no desire for David to be present, much less involved or influential in resolving the current dilemma that Israel's army faced.

In spite of Eliab's displeasure, word about David and his statements about Goliath reached the ears of the king. In response, like the prophet Samuel, Saul sent for him. David's confidence and faith did not wane in the presence of the king. David said to Saul:

> *Let no one lose heart on account of this Philistine; your servant will go and fight him.*
>
> 1 Samuel 17:32, NIV

What must have run through Saul's mind at that moment? Excitement and relief likely enveloped Saul when he first learned that there might actually be a man ready to confront Goliath. It had been days, even weeks of waiting. Now, one stood before him; one who may have been smaller than any of Saul's men, yet spoke with a confidence larger than that of the entire army of Israel!

With his hopes having been dashed against the jagged rocks of disappointment, Saul told David that he was no match for such a giant like Goliath. Saul had no reason for embracing David's confidence. David was just a boy, and Goliath had been a fighting man since his youth.

David was not shaken by Saul's evaluation of the situation. He related to Saul how, as a shepherd, he had faced lions and bears. When they laid hold of one of his father's sheep, he did more than chase them away; he rescued the sheep from their mouths. If that wasn't enough, David stated that when the wild animals turned on him, he killed them (1 Samuel 17:34-35)!

The fact that David simply remembered these events is not, in itself, significant. After all, who would not remember being in close proximity of a lion or a bear? Failing to remember such encounters would be more amazing than recalling them.

What is noteworthy about David's memory is that it served as a catalyst for faith for the present battle. David was not discouraged by Saul's assessment of him in comparison to Goliath. David had a powerful memory of how God had given him victory over obstacles in his past. When David looked at Goliath, he did not allow fear to cloud his memory of past victories. His powerful memory of God who enabled him to defeat lions and bears was his foundation of faith to defeat Goliath. David told Saul:

> *Your servant has killed both the lion and the bear; and this uncircumcised Philistine will be like one of them.*
> 1 Samuel 17:36

OVERCOMING PRESENT GIANTS BY REMEMBERING PAST VICTORIES

When we are facing a difficult situation, when we are confronted with what appears to be an unavoidable obstacle; one that appears to be way beyond our ability to overcome, when we are starring into the eyes of a "giant," are we consumed with fear, or do we draw faith from past victories? It seems to be human nature to quickly forget God's past victories in our lives when we are facing difficulties. How easy it is for us to become discouraged and hopeless in the midst of the battles of life.

When God delivered Israel from Egypt and led them through the wilderness to the Promised Land, the children of Israel experienced the miraculous hand of God. When caught between the Egyptian army and the Red Sea, God parted the waters. His people walked on dry ground while the Egyptians drowned. Yet, when they were in need of water, they complained! God miraculously provided all of the water that a vast number of people required. When they were in need of food, did they remember what God had done in the past? No. They grumbled and complained!

Before we become too critical of the children of Israel, let us examine our own heart. Whenever we find ourselves in the midst of a difficult situation, is our first response one of faith in light of God's faithfulness to us in the past, or is it one of complaining about the giant that is before us? All of us have experienced God's grace and victory in some way. Yet, how quickly we forget in the present what He has done in the past.

Perhaps, at some point, you found yourself in need of a small financial miracle. You saw no way of meeting this need yourself. In desperation, you cried out to God. Miraculously, a check comes in the mail that you did not expect, a check that just happened to be enough to meet your need. You rejoice and tell your friends about God's miraculous provision.

Several months later, you find yourself in need of another financial miracle. This one is twice as much as the one you faced earlier. Do you face this challenge filled with faith because God came through in the past, or do you find yourself saying, "I know God came through last time, but I'm not sure He will this time? This amount is so much larger than the last one." Even worse yet, do we face our present challenging circumstances failing even to remember what God has done for us in the past?

As we face our giant today, do we do so in faith because of victories in the past, or do we face them in fear as if God has never come through for us? Do we see our giant as being too big for God? Have we allowed difficulties to rob us of our confidence in God's ability to deliver us today as He has in the past?

When David faced Goliath, he could have succumbed to the same fear that gripped the army of Israel. As intimidating as a confrontation with a lion or a bear may have been for David, he could have allowed the thought of a battle with Goliath to be much more so. In the face of Goliath, David could have forgotten about, or ignored his past victories over lions and bears. He could have, but he didn't! David viewed his present obstacle with a powerful memory of past victories.

Are you doing the same? When you see the giant that stands between you and God's best for your life, are you filled with fear or are you full of faith? Are you forgetting all that God has already done for you in the past as you confront the present?

Does your giant appear to be bigger than your God? If it does, you are likely more focused on the giant than on God. Whatever we focus on becomes the biggest issue in our mind. If we are focused on the obstacle, it will "grow" in our minds. Our perspective of the obstacle will appear to be more and more insurmountable if we continue to focus on it.

As a young man, I remember someone telling me that you could block out the sun with a coin. At first, I thought the idea was ridiculous until he demonstrated how it was possible. If you hold up a coin between your eye and the sun at just the right distance between the two, the sun could be blocked from your vision by the coin. The rays of the sun around the coin would still be visible, but you could not see the sun itself.

Though the sun is immensely larger than a coin, one can lose sight of it if one's focus is on a coin. The same is true of the giants we face. No giant can compare with our God, but if we focus on our giants, they can appear to be larger than our God. They can even block our view of God altogether. When the twelve spies entered the Promised Land, two brought back a good report while ten brought back a negative one. All twelve saw the same land. The difference between their reports was determined by their focus. The two with a good report focused on the goodness of the land and God's promise that He would give it to them. The other ten had a different focus:

> *The land we explored devours those living in it. All the people we saw there are of great size ... we seemed like grasshoppers in our own eyes.*
> Numbers 13:32-33, NIV

Two spies focused on grapes; the other ten focused on giants. The people who heard both reports focused on the bad one instead of the good. They feared the giants, forgot God's past victory over Egypt and failed to believe God's Word. The result? They missed the Promised Land.

In this work, it is not my intent to make light of your situation. Many people have experienced painful childhoods as a result of abuse. Others have suffered through traumatic experiences at the hands of peers at school or work. The pain is real, the memories are fresh and the lies of the Enemy, as a result, are debilitating.

However, God is greater than any giant you will ever face. One of the best ways to defeat them is to focus on what God has done in the past to build your faith about what He can do in the present. Even if you cannot remember a victory in your own life sufficient to build your faith, the Bible is filled with examples of God's power and victory. You can build your faith by considering these examples. You are examining one right now, that of David's victory over Goliath.

Satan seeks to enlarge our giant by causing us to focus on it rather than God. The truth is, there is no giant that can compare with our great God! As the psalmist wrote, *"Great is our God and mighty in power"* (Psalm 147:5, NIV). There is none greater. If we focus on God, our giants will "shrink."

When it came to Goliath, David had a proper mindset. He saw Goliath from a spiritual perspective. He also had a powerful memory. Fresh in David's mind were his victories over lions and bears. In light of these, it did not matter how tall Goliath stood. Whether he was nine, ninety or nine hundred feet tall, Goliath was no match for David's great God. Your giant is not either! Let us now look at the third "stone" in David's pouch, his proven method.

Chapter Seven

DAVID'S PROVEN METHOD—A SLING AND A STONE

Whether it was David's confidence or the simple fact that there was no one else who was willing to fight that eventually motivated Saul to allow David to go into battle, we may never know. The Scripture only tells us that Saul said to David,

Go, and may the Lord be with you.
1 Samuel 17:37

Undoubtedly, Saul recognized that apart from God's involvement, David would never be successful.

The king desired to do what he could to help David prepare for combat. He offered David his armor and his sword. David dressed himself in Saul's armor and tried walking around while wearing it. The young shepherd quickly concluded that he could not go into battle dressed as he was. He told Saul:

I cannot go in these ... I am not used to them.
1 Samuel 17:39, NIV

Certainly, Saul's armor and sword were nowhere near as weighty as that of Goliath's. Nevertheless, compared to David's normal shepherd outfit and weapons, they were quite cumbersome. He also had no experience with either.

There was no time for David to grow into, or get used to Saul's armor. If David were to have any chance at victory, it would not be as a result of Saul's weapon or armor. There would have to be another option.

David removed Saul's armor. Then, he reached for more familiar items. The Scripture tells us that:

> *He took his staff in his hand, chose five smooth stones from the stream, put them in the pouch of his shepherd's bag and, with his sling in his hand, approached the Philistine.*
>
> 1 Samuel 17: 40, NIV

David's choice of weapons must have appeared to be futile, even foolish, to anyone who was present. Yet, they were what David had used in the past, what he was used to using. We have no record of David wielding anything else to protect his sheep or himself from lions and bears. His staff and his sling were likely the common tools of the trade of most, if not all shepherds in his day. As impotent as they may have appeared in the face of such a great giant, they were what David was used to, and thus, what David would take into battle.

Our Proven Methods

David's example requires us to ask the following question: "What 'weapons' should we take into battle against the giants we face?" As we are about to face our giant, will we be required to fight in a way that is unfamiliar to us, or can we go into battle with that which we have used in the past, that with which we, by God's grace, have been successful? Will God work through us as He has in the past or will we have to run to another to borrow what they have used? Has God already placed in our hands, what we need to fight bigger giants?

The enemy of our souls does not oppose us empty-handed. He has weapons with which he intends to harm us. Satan is a deceiver and a destroyer. He does not have our best interest in mind. The giants we face are weapons through which he seeks not only to hinder us but also to harm us. Most likely, this comes as no surprise to you. You know it all too well.

There were times when the Lord led Israel into battle to fight their enemies and defeat them. At other times, God gave Israel victory without them having to engage in conflict. The city of Jericho fell simply by Israel marching around its walls for seven days and ending their last march with a shout. Gideon defeated the Midianites with only 300 men, and none of them killed a single Midianite. All God required them to do was to smash jars, blow trumpets and hold torches as they shouted, *"A sword for the Lord and for Gideon"* (Judges 7:20).

It is true that at times God required His people to do little in order to defeat their foes. However, He rarely required them to do nothing. There were times when they were required to battle and times when they were commanded to do that which may have appeared to be of no military benefit at all. Yet, when they were obedient, God routed their enemies before them.

What we learn from these examples is that if we are obedient to His commands, He will give us the victory. As David declared to Goliath:

It is not by sword or spear that the Lord saves; for the battle is the Lord's.

1 Samuel 17:47

It is not the weapon, nor the warrior that brings victory. God is the one who defeats giants, but He does so through us and with the weapons He directs and gives us to use.

David went into battle with Goliath with a sling and stones. He did not do so because they were the weapons best suited for killing giants, but because they were the weapons with which he was familiar. God had given David victory in the past with nothing more; and with God, he believed he would be no less victorious with them against Goliath.

What does this tell us about our battles against giants? David's sling and stones reveal that **we will not win our battles with someone else's armor. We will win the battle over our giants with that which God has taught us,** and that which He commands us to use. In our Christian experience, God will teach us how to engage in spiritual battles on a smaller scale before calling upon us to tackle bigger obstacles. What we learn in these smaller battles are valuable lessons that prepare us for larger challenges. Let's return to the simple example that we talked about earlier regarding financial issues.

You find yourself needing to pay a bill of less than one hundred dollars without knowing how you will be able to do so. Recognizing your need for Him in this situation, you call out to God in prayer, and seek direction from His Word. The next morning you find yourself reading a passage in Matthew about God clothing the lilies of the field and feeding the birds of the air. You sense the Lord speaking to your heart, and you begin to pray: "Lord if you care about birds and flowers, I believe you care about me. I choose not to doubt your faithfulness to me and ask you to meet my financial need. I trust that you will do so."

Two days later, an unexpected check comes in the mail that is enough to cover the bill you had prayed about and believed God to meet. You realize that the best way to respond to this type of need in the future is not by worrying but by seeking God in prayer and His Word. Several months go by, and you find yourself facing another financial issue. This time it involves an amount far greater than one hundred dollars. You have been faithful with your giving and have been spending wisely, but an unexpected car repair will cost you far more than what is in your budget.

What do you do? You begin by doing what you did the last time you had a financial need. Though the need is far greater, unless the Lord leads you otherwise, simply do what you've done in the past. Seek God in prayer and through His Word. It may require more time in prayer and more faith than before. After all, that is how we grow. However, it may not require any new "weapons," just the ones we're familiar with; the ones we're used to using. Does this remind you of David?

When we find ourselves confronted by giants, fear may grip our hearts. We know how to fight small battles, but certainly not giants! Our fear may drive us to search for "weapons" that others possess; that we believe will be more powerful than those we've fought with in the past. We can learn from others, but the best time to do so is usually not in the heat of the battle unless they are battling along side of us.

Though we can learn from others who have had success in spiritual warfare, God may call us to fight differently.

Through our own experiences, God has taught us what he has for a reason. Most likely, in the midst of our struggles with giants, the Holy Spirit will remind us of how God had given us victory in the past. New battles may require new weapons, but oftentimes, God will lead us to fight with that which we have tested and those through which He has brought us victory in the past.

David's weapons appeared to be useless against a giant like Goliath. Yet God used them to bring him down. **When God uses the improbable to accomplish the "impossible," He receives all the glory!** Paul said that God has chosen to use the "foolishness" of preaching to reach those who are lost in sin (1Cor. 1:21). Our weapons may appear puny, but they are powerful to the pulling down of strongholds. They are spiritual in nature and effective against the enemy (2 Corinthians 10:4). Whatever God calls you to use to defeat your giant, it will be superior to anything anyone else has to offer you. You don't need Saul's armor to defeat your giant. There may be no need for you to learn any new tactics to gain the victory. It may just be a matter of relying on God and fighting with the "sling and stones" that He has already put in your hand. It is now time to discover David's fourth "stone," his propelling momentum.

Chapter Eight

DAVID'S PROPELLING MOMENTUM—WORDS AND ACTIONS OF FAITH

Into the battle with Goliath, David brought a proper mindset; he viewed his giant from a spiritual perspective, not from a physical one. He was equipped with a powerful memory; he recalled how God had delivered him from lions and bears. David was also armed with a proven method for victory. He did not need any of Saul's armor or weapons; he knew how to battle with stones and a sling. They brought him success in the past, and they would be sufficient for what he now faced. As efficacious as these three alone may have been, David held two more "stones" for battle. Beyond his proper mindset, his powerful memory, and his proven method, David possessed a propelling momentum for battle. In the face of potentially discouraging words, David moved forward, propelled by words and actions of faith.

The Scripture states that after Saul had agreed to allow David to fight Goliath, he approached the Philistine giant with his sling in hand and stones in his bag. David was ready and willing to take on the one others were unwilling to fight. The battle was about to begin.

Goliath's Verbal Attack

The king of Israel may have been relieved that there was at least one person with determination and faith to battle Goliath. Saul may have even been encouraged by David's confidence, but Goliath was unimpressed. As David approached the giant, his boldness and confidence encountered Goliath's disdain and displeasure. One can only imagine what Goliath's first impressions were of the "mighty warrior" that Israel had sent to confront him. Unlike Goliath, there was little, if anything, about David's appearance and experience that would have intimidated Goliath. In fact, it was quite the opposite! David was just a boy. Scripture states that he was a handsome boy, but just a boy. Physical attractiveness may be an effective weapon for winning a battle for a woman's heart, but it is ineffectual in a battle with a giant.

As David approached Goliath, the giant made known his disgust with the situation. Goliath said to David: *"Am I a dog, that you come to me with sticks?"* (1 Samuel 17:43). Not only was Goliath unimpressed with David and his weapons, he saw both as an affront to his strength and ability. One would assume that any army, after properly assessing their opponent, would send forth a worthy warrior equipped with whatever was necessary to have a legitimate chance at victory. When Goliath saw David with nothing but the apparatus of a shepherd, he took it personally. In the eyes of Goliath, Israel had humiliated him by sending a boy into battle, and, in his perspective, David had mocked him by approaching him with nothing more than a shepherd's rod and sling.

For forty days Goliath successfully taunted and defied Israel. For forty days, Israel cowered in fear. At last, Israel finally sent forth a contender, one who was willing to put an end to their shame and humiliation. Whom did they send? They sent a mere youth, a shepherd, with a stick, stones, and a sling. Those who had been afraid to engage Goliath in battle appeared to be unafraid to attack his pride and insult his ability. By sending out David, they had stirred the giant!

Goliath was ready to end this embarrassment quickly. He said to David, *"Come here ... and I will give your flesh to the birds of the air and the beasts of the field"* (1 Samuel 17:44, NIV). Before a spear was thrown or a stone was slung, Goliath hurled demeaning words that revealed his desire to defeat David. There was no doubt as to Goliath's intentions. In light of the perceived disrespect shown to him on the part of Israel, Goliath addressed his opponent in a way that offered David no dignity, nor did he intend to show David any mercy.

DAVID'S RESPONSE

David had arrived at a pivotal point in his encounter with Goliath. Up to this moment, he was filled with faith, not fear. He spoke boldly and confidently about what God had done in the past and how he would be able to defeat Goliath. He was not intimidated by Israel's paralysis to move forward. Neither Goliath's size and experience nor Saul's timidity and initial reluctance to send him into battle shook David's confidence. Though only a youth and much smaller than Goliath, David stood tall in his conviction that he could overcome his giant.

Now, David was no longer in the presence of his people. He was face to face with Goliath. This giant that confronted him was not about to run. Goliath did not fear David. To the contrary, his very presence provoked Goliath. Had Goliath lacked any motivation, zeal or incentive to defeat one of Israel's best, it had been fanned into full flame at the sight of David. Goliath's words left no doubt in David's mind as to what the giant intended to do to him.

What would David do at this moment? He had jumped every hurdle, maneuvered through every obstacle, and endured every dispiriting word from his brother and Saul. Would this final onslaught on David's faith by Goliath's discouraging diatribe be enough to stop him short of engaging and defeating his giant? Would David's previous faith for victory now falter? Now that David was face to face with the giant, would Goliath's words become a prophetic declaration as a result of fear on the part of David?

If David's faith had given way at that moment, every bit of confidence that he displayed previously would have been in vain. No matter how sure David was of victory up to this point, if he let Goliath's discouraging words penetrate his heart, David's stone would never penetrate the giant's forehead. In order for David to overcome his giant, he would need to get past this last verbal attack and engage in battle, not timidly but boldly. How would he do so?

DAVID'S VERBAL RESPONSE

The Scriptures tell us how David responded to the defiant words of Goliath. David boldly proclaimed:

You come against me with sword and spear and javelin, but I come against you in the name of the

Lord Almighty, the God of the armies of Israel, whom you have defied. This day the Lord will hand you over to me, and I'll strike you down and cut off your head.
1 Samuel 17:45-46, NIV

David responded to Goliath's discouraging words with a verbal declaration of faith. David did not simply reject what Goliath had said; he answered him with words to the contrary. David could have just ignored what was spoken against him. However, that may not have been enough to restore the atmosphere of victory. David chose instead, to speak about the victory he planned to accomplish against Goliath.

Goliath declared that he would feed David's dead body to the *"birds of the air and the beasts of the field"* (1 Samuel 17:44). When David spoke with King Saul, he told him how God had delivered him in the past from the beasts of the field. As we saw earlier, David had a powerful memory. God had delivered him in the past, and David believed He would do so again. Instead of swallowing Goliath's words, he declared that not only Goliath but the entire army of the Philistines would face the outcome that Goliath said David would experience:

Today I will give the carcasses of the Philistine army to the birds of the air and the beasts of the earth.
1 Samuel 17:46, NIV

Goliath's fearful prediction did not send him running or retreating. Neither was David frozen in place by Goliath's threats. David neither ran nor stood still. He did not flee or freeze. Instead, he declared what he believed would be the outcome of their confrontation. He stated that what Goliath had declared to be the future fate of David, would actually be the experience of the Philistine army. David was not discouraged, distracted or deterred by Goliath's words. Instead, he spoke words of faith and readied himself for battle.

David's Source of Confidence

Before we consider how David's response to Goliath's words can help us defeat the giants we face in our lives, it would be wise to consider the source of David's confidence. David did not draw faith from a positive attitude, a youthful exuberance or a smooth rock from a stream. David's faith and confidence came from His God.

In response to Goliath, David said:

You come against me with a sword, a spear, and javelin, but I come against you in the name of the Lord.

1 Samuel 17:45, NIV

Notice that David first listed Goliath's weapons. Then he told Goliath about his weapon, the name of the Lord. By his statement, David revealed that his confidence and faith was not placed in any physical weapon but His powerful God! Against that weapon, no weapon, not even one in the hand of a giant, was any match!

During his lifetime, David wrote many psalms. We read of his musical ability in the same book of the Bible that contains the account of David and Goliath. When the spirit of the Lord left Saul, the scripture states that *"an evil spirit from the Lord tormented him"* (1 Samuel 16:14). David was called upon to bring relief of Saul's torment from this evil spirit through his gift of music. The Bible tells us that when the evil spirit came upon Saul:

David would take his harp and play. Then relief would come to Saul.
1 Samuel 16:23, NIV

The book of Psalms contains many of David's songs, including Psalm 20, where David states:

Some trust in chariots and some in horses, but we will trust in the name of the Lord our God.
Psalm 20:7, NIV

As king, David experienced many victories over his enemies. He saw the hand of God defeat powerful armies. He knew the history of his people, how God delivered them from Egypt. Israel walked on dry land through the Red Sea, but the Egyptians drowned in it. The song of Moses and Miriam declares:

Pharaoh's chariots and his army he has hurled into the sea.
Exodus 15:4, NIV

If chariots were no match for David's God, what was there to fear of Goliath's weapons of war? Nothing! Even though they were much larger than those of a normal-sized warrior, David was not intimidated by Goliath's sword, spear or javelin. David didn't need a man-made weapon in order to overcome his giant; he went into battle with the most powerful weapon, the name of the Lord!

THE BATTLE WITHIN THE BATTLE
WHOSE WORDS WILL YOU BELIEVE?

Words are powerful. They can inspire faith. Paul said that faith comes by hearing and hearing by the Word, or the preaching of Christ (Romans 10:17). Taking hold of truth that is spoken, or embracing an encouraging word, can instill great faith.

Words can also produce fear. For example, when the twelve spies returned from the Promised Land, two of them gave a positive report about the produce of the Land. They also spoke of God's ability and promise to give it to them. However, ten of the spies brought a negative report. Regarding those living in the Land, they said, *"We can't attack these people; they are stronger than we are"* (Numbers 13:31, NIV). Listen to how they described the giants who inhabited the Land: *"We seemed like grasshoppers in our own eyes, and we looked the same to them"* (Numbers 13:33, NIV).

The people ignored the good report, and instead, chose to believe the negative one. They received the words of those who spoke with fear rather than those spoken with faith. Their choice resulted in a failure to believe God's Word that He would give them the Land.

There is much we can learn from the way David dealt with Goliath's verbal assault. The first lesson is that, like Goliath, the giant we face will make every effort to discourage us, and the discouragement will often come in the form of negative or threatening words.

The words may enter our ears from the lips of people or simply be whispered into our minds by the enemy. However we "hear" them, the goal of these words is to discourage us from battling and overcoming the giants we face. Not only should we expect this kind of attack at some point during our struggle, we would be wise to expect them to come moments before we engage in battle. In fact, **discouraging words are hurled at us just before victory is within our reach.** It is often the last attempt of the enemy to keep us from breaking through to freedom.

In the Scriptures, there are a number of descriptive words and defining terms that are used to describe our ultimate enemy, Satan. Jesus called him the *"father of lies."* A discussion that occurred between some Jewish religious leaders and Jesus is found in John 8. Part of the verbal exchange dealt with whether these Jewish leaders were true descendants of Abraham as they had professed to be. Jesus challenged their claim based on the fact that they had not conducted themselves as genuine sons of Abraham. Jesus declared that their actions were more like those of Satan. In defense of His statement, Jesus described the nature and activity of Satan. He stated that Satan "does not stand in the truth because there is no truth in him." Jesus went on to say:

> *Whenever he speaks a lie, he speaks from his own nature, for he is a liar and the father of lies.*
> John 8:44

From these words of Jesus, we learn two truths regarding the ultimate giant we face. The first is that Satan is not silent; he speaks. He spoke to Adam and Eve in the Garden. He spoke to Jesus when he tempted Him in the wilderness. We have clear scriptural evidence that Satan speaks. The second truth is that Satan is a liar. When Satan speaks, he speaks lies, for he speaks out of his own nature.

In contrast, Jesus speaks truth. He said that He was *"the way, and the truth, and the life"* (John 14:6). One way to distinguish the voice of God and the voice of Satan is that Jesus always speaks the truth, and Satan always speaks lies. Satan may quote Scripture, but he will do so in a deceptive and perverse way, thus distorting truth into a lie.

Jesus' description of Satan as the father of lies indicates that he is the source of all that is untrue. Therefore, any and all lies originate with him. You may be hearing the words of a relative, a friend or an enemy, but if it is a lie, its source is Satan.

This is not to say that everyone who lies is under Satan's direct control. When Peter told Jesus that He should not be crucified, Jesus responded by saying, *"Get behind me, Satan"* (Matthew 16:23). The Lord's rebuke of Peter is not evidence that Peter was under the control of Satan. After all, Jesus had just told Peter that his profession of Him as the Christ was the result of the work of the Holy Spirit. Jesus simply recognized the words of Peter as an attempt to keep Him from doing what the Father had sent Him to do, and the one who ultimately desired to keep Him from obeying His Father was Satan.

Believing and Speaking Words of Faith

So what does all this have to do with our giants? Everything! Like Goliath, our giants desire to keep us under their control through lies and deception. The result will be a failure on our part to move forward into all God has for us.

We may not recognize them as lies. In fact, they often sound like truth to us. There may indeed be some element of truth to what we hear. It is much easier to deceive a person by mixing a "little" lie within a batch of truth to disguise it. That is what makes the enemy's words so deceiving. If you swallow a lie, you run the risk of believing something that isn't true about yourself and your ability to overcome the giant opposing you.

A lie becomes "truth" to anyone who believes it to be true. How many people live their lives believing that something is true that is not? Deception is a powerful tool.

Lies have a way of appearing to be true due to personal experiences. When a person has an emotionally or physically painful experience, shortly after that traumatic or embarrassing moment, the enemy plants thoughts about God, themselves or others in their minds and hearts. There may be little or no truth to the thought, but the painful experience makes the lie easier to accept as truth.

For example, a woman molested as a child by a relative, believes that she is "dirty" and undeserving of love. Why? Because that is what she had been told. A father continually struggles to provide for his family because he cannot seem to keep a job. Why? As a boy, his father often told him that he never did anything right. Whenever he has to learn a new job, he fails to catch on;

not because he lacks ability, but because he believes the lie that he was told as a boy. He believes the lie that he is unable to do anything right, and his belief about himself keeps him from finding success at anything.

When any lie becomes deeply lodged within people's hearts, they begin to live out that lie in their everyday lives. When they do, their actions and what they experience as a result of their actions have a way of "validating" and further embedding the lie within their hearts. The lie is reinforced; not because it is true, but because their belief that it is true affects how they think and act, thus providing "evidence" for the lie being true. How sinister is this whole matter of lies and deception!

What lies have been spoken that you have erroneously embraced as truth? You may not be able to think of any at this moment, but that does not mean you do not believe any. It's not surprising that a person finds it difficult to identify a lie that they believe for the simple reason that they believe what they believe to be the truth. This is why it can be so difficult for us to overcome giants that are based on a lie. When a person believes a lie to be true, it requires a revelation of God to recognize that what they believe is a lie.

The only way to break the power of lies and deception is receiving the truth. Any giant that gains its foothold through a lie can only be defeated when one recognizes and embraces the truth. Truth is found in Jesus, and we need a revelation of Him to recognize the truth. Truth is not found in every experience of life or every word that has been said to you, and it certainly is not found in the whisperings of Satan.

Lies must be overcome with truth, and **it is often the spoken words of truth that break the power of lies.** Satan spoke to Jesus in the wilderness. Jesus was not silent in return. He responded with truth. The implication in the Bible is that Jesus not only thought but also spoke words of truth in response to Satan's temptations.

The power of the spoken word can be found not only in the temptation of Jesus in the Gospels but throughout Scripture. The Bible clearly states that God spoke the world into existence (Genesis 1:3-26). Jesus taught His disciples about the power of faith and the spoken word when He cursed the fig tree (Matthew 21:18-22). The book of Proverbs states that life and death are in the power of the tongue (Proverbs 18:21). James 3 warns us about the power of the tongue with its positive and negative potential.

It is not the purpose of this work to explore this matter in greater detail. What is important for the subject at hand is that David overcame Goliath's discouraging and potentially debilitating words by speaking words of faith. His words were not a mere exercise in positive thinking. He did say what he said in an effort to psyche himself up for battle. David was not engaging in a personal "pep talk" like those common among sports teams.

David was addressing his giant in a way that let Goliath know that he was not discouraged by his words. David did not accept the giant's words as truth. David declared what he knew to be true in the face of his giant's lies. David declared what he believed God was going to do to Goliath through him. As a result, David did not run away from the battle; he ran into the battle. David's words of faith provided him with a propelling momentum to move forward and attack the giant he faced.

If we are going to overcome our giants, we will likely find ourselves needing to resist discouraging words, negative thoughts, and deceptive beliefs. In the face of such onslaughts, we will be required to speak the truth in the face of lies and deception. Do not believe what the enemy has told you in the past or what the enemy is telling you as you are about to engage in battle. **Your giant will do everything possible to discourage you, especially as you get closer to victory.**

Goliath was not able to keep David from entering the battlefield. His presence and taunts kept the army of Israel at bay, but he was unsuccessful in deterring David. David did not succumb to fear. There he was, facing Goliath. All that Goliath had left in his arsenal was his threat to kill David and feed him to the birds and animals. It was David's last opportunity to run from the battle. At that very moment, he could choose either to fight or to flee. David chose to fight. The actual battle was about to begin, but it may be said that the outcome was already determined by David's words of faith in the face of Goliath's threat.

In our struggle with our giants, if we truly seek to defeat them, we will face a moment of truth. The time will come when we will stand "face to face" with that which has hindered our Christian walk for months, for years, maybe even for decades! When we do, our giant may shout out one last defiant and daunting threat. At that moment, we will have the choice to either fight or flee. Our words may be the first indication of which choice we will make. If we give in to doubt and fear, we may flee, but if we declare God's truth, we will be ready for battle. Your victory will be within reach!

Chapter Nine

DAVID'S PURE MOTIVE —GOD'S GLORY!

We know that David was not intimidated by Goliath's threatening words. Goliath was not concerned about what David said in response, though he arguably should have been. The Scripture tells us that after their verbal exchange, Goliath moved toward David. Like a giant-killer, *"David ran quickly toward the battle line to meet the Philistine"* (1 Samuel 17:48). Wait! Before we get to the actual battle, there is yet one more "stone" that David possessed that cannot be ignored. This final stone may well be the most essential of them all. To discover the final weapon of David's spiritual arsenal, we must consider something else that David said to Goliath just before engaging him in battle.

For God's Glory

As he stood before Goliath, David not only boldly proclaimed that he would defeat him but also the entire Philistine army. In no uncertain terms, David not only declared what he was going to do but also his motivation for doing what he said he would do. **David's words make it clear that his motive had nothing to do with personal honor, fame or glory.**

When he first arrived at the battle, David had asked

what would be done for the one who defeated Goliath. King Saul had promised great wealth, along with his daughter in marriage to the one who overcame Goliath. He also promised to excuse the victor's family from taxes. (In today's world, the exemption from taxes might have been the best of the three!) Saul's offer was both lucrative and prestigious. It included financial security and a prominent position to the one qualified to receive them.

As great as the king's offer was for the victor, no one was willing to take the challenge, not even David, at least not for those reasons. As honorable and profitable as the king's promises were, David's motivation was not personal enrichment or family favor. His zeal for defeating Goliath had nothing to do with personal fame or gain. When David declared to Goliath why he was going to defeat him, he said that it was so that *"the whole world will know that there is a God in Israel"* (1 Samuel 17:46, NIV).

David saved the best weapon for last. This last "stone" of David, his desire for God to be glorified as a result of his victory over Goliath, is paramount to all the others. David possessed a proper mindset. He saw Goliath from a spiritual perspective. He had a powerful memory; David remembered how God had delivered him from lions and bears. In addition, David owned a proven method for victory. His staff, his sling and his God had been all he needed in the past, and they would be enough against Goliath as well. Added to these was David's propelling momentum. The discouraging and threatening words of Goliath had reached David's ears, but they did not penetrate his heart. David did not allow fear to take hold; in the face of threats, he spoke words of faith. David told Goliath that he would be the one that would be fed to the birds of the air and the beasts of the field.

As effective as these weapons were, David's best was his pure motive. The one whom the Bible describes as a man after God's own heart had a pure motive for victory. He desired to see God glorified. That was David's motive. It was his pure motive that inspired him to take on and overcome the giant named Goliath.

A Self–Centered World

We live in a self-centered world. That is not a judgmental statement; it is simply an accurate description of the human condition apart from Christ. The fallen-nature of mankind is bent toward self-preservation, self-will, and selfish pursuits.

It began with Lucifer's desire to ascend to become like God. He was not content to remain in the position that God had created Him to hold. He wanted more. He wanted God's glory.

There is a well-known portion of the book of Isaiah that many theologians believe reveals the prideful and selfish desire of Satan. In the fourteenth chapter of this book, we find these words:

You said in your heart, "I will ascend to heaven; I will raise my throne above the stars of God; I will sit enthroned upon the mount of the assembly ... I will ascend the tops of the clouds; I will make myself like the Most High."

Isaiah 14:13-14, NIV

Lucifer's selfish desire to ascend actually resulted in

him being cast down from the position in which God had placed him. In the Garden, he successfully deceived Eve into embracing his self-centered nature, disobeying God's command and pursuing a pernicious path of personal promotion. Satan told Eve that eating from the tree from which God had forbidden them to eat would make them wise.

Then came the truly self-centered deception: Eve would be like God! (Genesis 3:5). That should sound familiar. The prideful, self-centered heart that Lucifer manifested in his attempt to become like God was birthed in Eve as a result of his temptation. Eve was deceived into disobedience. Adam was not deceived; he simply disobeyed God. The Scripture states: *"She also gave some to her husband ... and he ate"* (Genesis 3:6, NIV). The pride of Satan had now infiltrated the heart of Adam and Eve. Over time it has permeated throughout the entire human race.

The Bible is filled with examples of humanity's selfish desire for wealth, fame, power, and position. Secular history is replete with it as well. The lust of the flesh, the lust of the eyes and the pride of life that John speaks of in his first letter, have not waned over time; instead, they have flourished! At times it is easily detectable in the words and actions of those selfishly seeking to rise in power or prominence. In other cases, it is more concealed, even wrapped in what appears to be benevolent intentions and desires. However, time and testing often uncover the true motives of an individual, and they are often self-serving.

That is not to say that there are not well-meaning or genuine attempts, both within religious and non-religious circles, on the part of some to serve others with little or no regard for personal attention or benefit. It is simply undeniable that, like a car whose alignment is in need of adjustment, the fallen nature of mankind pulls in the direction of selfish ambition and self-exaltation. It is just how fallen nature is bent.

A God-Centered Warrior

David's world was no different than ours in this regard. One might even argue that Saul's offer to reward the one who would fight and defeat Goliath appealed to this human condition of self-benefit. Though David's heart was not impervious to this deep-seated human passion, it played no part in his decision to fight Goliath. To the contrary, David's desire was God's glory, not his own.

Consider for a moment, what might have gone through David's heart after becoming aware of this challenge by Goliath had it been filled with self-promotion and glory. Had David's desire to become king of Israel been one of self-centeredness, he might have viewed a battle with Goliath as a great opportunity. No one was willing to fight Goliath, not even the king! This may be David's best chance to distinguish himself from every other military person in Israel.

Boldly stating that he was willing to take on this formidable opponent would not go unnoticed. He could have played that moment for all it was worth. His courage and bravery would become evident to everyone. Granted, few if any, would believe he could or would be victorious. Those doubtful opinions would only make his victory that much more impressive. As far as physical stature is concerned, David did not tower over others like Saul or his brother Eliab, but a victory over Goliath would place him head and shoulders above the crowd. Surely, it would only be a matter of time before the nation would install him as king.

David could have cemented his own destiny with a victory over Goliath, but what if he lost? If David had been thinking selfishly about his future, losing a battle with Goliath would potentially end his chances of ever becoming king—to say nothing of his life—that is, if it was up to him to make it happen. For David, there was a tremendous upside to a victory over the giant, but the downside was even greater due to the simple fact that defeat was much more probable. David could be humiliated for going into battle. Worse yet, he could die. In either case, becoming king would be unlikely if not impossible. If David was thinking only of himself, fighting Goliath may not have been worth the risk.

But David's motive for going into battle with Goliath was anything but self-centered. He was willing to risk it all: his reputation, his future, even his very life. David did not cower in the face of the Philistine for fear of any personal loss. His own personal welfare was not on his mind. He saw an uncircumcised Philistine who was taunting, not just himself or the army of Israel, but the armies of the living God. David's pure motive for victory would not allow him to stand for that! David had to fight Goliath. The world needed to know that there was a God in Israel. That was David's pure motive for taking on Goliath.

Your Motive for Victory

After being made aware of David's pure motive for victory

over Goliath, we would be wise to examine our own hearts. Ask yourself this question: What is your overarching motive for desiring to overcome the giant you face? Is your motive a sincere desire for God's glory to be revealed, or do you simply want a more stress-free life? Are we seeking victory for the praise of the One who will set us free, or do we just want to find some rest from this life-long struggle? Before we engage our giant, we must ask ourselves this question: "Do we possess the same pure motive for overcoming our giant as David?" How we answer this question may make all the difference in the outcome of the battle.

As we consider our own desire for victory, it is imperative that we also recognize God's desire for us regarding the giants we face. God desires to give us victory over, and to set us free from, the giant we face. In Luke's Gospel, we find an account from the early days of Jesus' public ministry. The writer tells us that Jesus entered a synagogue in which he was handed a scroll. Upon the scroll were written the words of the prophet Isaiah. Jesus found and read the following passage:

> *The Spirit of the Lord is upon me because he has anointed me to preach good news to the poor. He has sent me to proclaim freedom for the prisoners and recovery of sight to the blind, to release the oppressed, to proclaim the year of our Lord's favor.*
> Luke 4:18-19, NIV

After reading these words, Jesus declared, *"Today this Scripture is fulfilled in your hearing"* (Luke 4:21). What Jesus proclaimed is that He had come to set people free from sickness, demonic oppression and anything that held them captive, anything that prevented them from experiencing all that God had for them. His life and ministry was spent, not only in teaching people but also healing them, casting out evil spirits and setting them free. In other words, Jesus came to overcome giants.

Knowing God's desire for us regarding the giants we face is critical to our victory. If we don't grasp the truth that God desires us to be victorious, we may never engage in the battle. We may never face our giant and fight them, much less, overcome them. **God's will for us is the same as it was for David; He desires for us to overcome our giants.**

God desires to set us free from that which is holding us back. Our desire for victory is to be His glory. His glory is to be our pure motive for desiring to overcome our giant. There is nothing wrong with wanting to be free from the things that the enemy has used to keep us from God's plans and purposes. The Scriptures tell us that Jesus, at times, asked people what they desired before He ministered to their need. It is not wrong to ask God for victory. We should long for it, even pursue it!

The issue is not whether God desires us to be victorious, nor whether we desire to overcome the giants we face, it is a matter of whether God's glory is our primary motive. When God gives us victory, will we glorify Him or will we be like the nine lepers who never returned to thank Him? After our giant is defeated, will we glorify God or simply inappreciably enjoy our liberty?

David's motivation for battling Goliath was not one of selfishness. David had a far greater motive than personal gain or fame; he wanted the world to know that there was a God in Israel. If we possess the pure motive for victory like David, we will also defeat our giant!

Chapter Ten

GOLIATH'S SWORD IN OUR HAND—OUR TESTIMONY

Let us now return for the conclusion of the battle between David and Goliath. After their verbal exchange, Goliath approached David. As he did, David did not run from Goliath. Instead, *"David ran quickly toward the battle line to meet the Philistine"* (1 Samuel 17:48).

Then David reached into his pouch, clasped a stone in his hand and placed it in his sling. With all the skill of an experienced shepherd, coupled with the anointing of the Shepherd, David slung the stone at Goliath. The stone *"sank into his forehead, and he fell facedown on the ground"* (1 Samuel 17:49, NIV). The Philistine giant fell at David's feet. David had overcome his giant.

There is yet more to be gleaned from this event if we are to fully appreciate, and adequately glorify God when He gives us victory over our giants. With Goliath on the ground, the Scripture tells us that David stood over him. He then *"took hold of the Philistine's sword and drew it from the scabbard. After he killed him, he cut off his head with his sword"* (1 Samuel 17:51, NIV).

The Scripture seems to be quite clear that David had killed Goliath with his sling and a stone. Yet, David removed Goliath's sword and used it to cut off the giant's head. There must be some reason why David did so. Perhaps David simply wanted to make sure that the giant was dead, never to taunt Israel again. Maybe he saw it as the just "reward" for one who had defied the army of the living God.

Whatever David's reason for doing what he did, there is a significant spiritual truth typified by David's action that applies to our battle with the giant we face. To remove the head of Goliath, David wielded the very sword that Goliath intended to use to destroy him! God removed Goliath's sword from his possession and placed it in the hand of David. What does this tell us about the victory God has for us over our giants? **God can take the very weapon Satan has used against us and put it in our hand as a sword to defeat him in the lives of others. That sword is the word of our testimony.** That which Satan sought to use to destroy us becomes our testimony of God's victory. It becomes a weapon, not in the hand of our enemy but in our hand to defeat him! When God gives us victory over our giant, we can share our testimony with others, declaring the victory God has given us! As we share our testimony, God is glorified! As others hear it and gain the faith to defeat their giants, God is glorified again!

Your victory over your giant will lead to others experiencing a similar victory. The Bible tells us that when the Philistines saw their slain warrior, they turned and ran (1 Samuel 17:51). When they did, *"The men of Israel and Judah arose and shouted and pursued the Philistines as far as the valley, and to the gates of Ekron"* (1 Samuel 17:52). After defeating Goliath, David was not the only one willing to battle that day. His victory over Goliath inspired the army of Israel to pursue their enemy, and pursue them they did!

David's victory over Goliath did more than inspire people on that day, it inspired others, years later. In the twenty-first chapter of the book of 2 Samuel, we again find Israel and the Philistines at war. David, with his men, went down to battle the Philistines, but the Scripture states something quite different about David here than it did when he faced Goliath. We learn that David *"became exhausted"* (2 Samuel 21:15).

What is similar between the two accounts is that a giant intended to take David's life. In this account, the giant's name was Ishi-Benob, described as *"one of the descendants of Rapha, whose bronze spearhead weighed three-hundred shekels"* (2 Samuel 21:16, NIV). David did not battle and defeat this foe. The Bible tells us that, *"Abishai son of Zeruiah came to David's rescue; he struck the Philistine down and killed him"* (2 Samuel 21:17, NIV). At this point in his life, David was not the young fighter who had defeated Goliath. However, it is likely that his past victory over Goliath set an example for another to follow.

Abishai was not the only brave warrior who was likely inspired by David; there were several others. This same chapter of 2 Samuel speaks of a man named *Sibbicai* who killed a giant named Saph who also was a descendant of Rapha. In another battle, we read of Elhanan, a man who killed *"Goliath the Gittite, who had a spear with a shaft like a weaver's rod"* (2 Samuel 17:19). Based on his description, this giant named Goliath was likely comparable to the one David had slain earlier. Then there was another descendant of Rapha, described as a huge man with six fingers and six toes on each hand and foot. Like the Goliath that David faced as a young shepherd, he too taunted Israel. When he did so, *"Jonathan son of Shimeah, David's brother, killed him"* (2 Samuel 21:21, NIV).

All four of these enemies of Israel are described as descendants of Rapha in Gath. The giant that David killed was also from Gath. It appears that the four foes spoken about in 2 Samuel were likely related, in some way to Goliath, whom David had defeated. David was not at a place in his life where he could battle these giants as he did Goliath. However, it is hard to believe that David's past victory did not inspire the men who were. Though David did not fight them, the Scripture states, *"they fell at the hands of David and his men"* (2 Samuel 21:22, NIV). David is actually credited with the victories over these giants along with those who fought and killed them. His victory over Goliath played a significant role in future victories. David set an example. He paved the way. David's victory over Goliath led to more victories by the hands of others who were close to David, and more giants were defeated because of his past victory.

Herein lies another way in which our victory over the giants we face can be for God's glory; our victory will encourage and empower others to take on and defeat the giants they face. Our testimony of victory not only glorifies God in that we acknowledge Him as the One who won the victory, our testimony will stir faith in the hearts of others who face giants. God will lead you to those battling the same type of giants you've battled. The Lord will use your story to bring hope to others, helping them to realize that victory over giants is possible. Your experience will declare to them that subservience to giants is not their only option. As you share your story, it will act as a sword to overcome demonic opposition and strongholds, allowing others to move forward in their faith!

Your victory over your giant will not only impact those around you; it has the potential of influencing future generations. Sin has a pernicious way of finding footholds within family lines. Tragically, we often hear of abusive parents having children who themselves grow up to abuse theirs. Drug, alcohol and sexual addictions often permeate from one generation to another. You may need to battle such "generational giants" somewhere along your path to God's best for you.

But sin is not alone in its ability to affect people from different generations. Your victory can also lay a new foundation of freedom upon which future generations can build. God's victory in your life over demonic strongholds can break what is often referred to as "generational curses." By overcoming your giants, you can, in essence, "replant your family tree" in the soil of blessing and breakthrough. The curses from the past can be broken, and a new pattern can begin when you courageously battle and beat the giants you face.

When it comes to overcoming giants, there is more at stake than your personal deliverance. Certainly, God wants us to be free of the enemy's grip. He desires your liberty, and He is glorified by your victory. However, God will receive greater glory when you share your testimony and help others overcome their giants. God will set you free in order that you might declare what He has done for you so that others may be set free as well

The man from whom Jesus had cast out a legion of demons desired to follow Him. In fact, he begged Jesus to allow him to do so. Jesus did not honor his request. Instead, he told the man to, *"Return home and tell how much God has done for you"* (Luke 8:39, NIV).

This man, who was now set free, had spent many years in his condition of bondage. He was a slave to the demonic activity that possessed him. There is little doubt that those among whom he lived were well aware of his miserable condition.

Now, he was free because of Jesus. It is understandable that this man would want to follow the One who broke the power of darkness over and in his life. Jesus called others to follow Him, but He desired this man to return to those who knew him and declare what Jesus did for him. We are not told whether this former demon-possessed man obeyed the Lord's command. We can assume that he did; and as he shared his testimony of deliverance, God was glorified.

In the same way, we should not keep our victory to ourselves. Our testimony has the power to stir faith in others to defeat their giants. If your motive for victory is for God to be glorified, you will take the weapon that the enemy sought to destroy you with and wield it as a sword! You will share your testimony of victory to help others defeat their giant!

Chapter Eleven

JESUS—THE SON OF DAVID
JESUS—THE "GIANT-KILLER"

The biblical account of David and Goliath has much to teach us about overcoming obstacles to our spiritual progress. Though this is the case, we must never forget that you and I can only be victorious if we rely upon the One who is the ultimate "giant-killer," Jesus. **The victory of Jesus over Satan is what makes our victory over giants possible.**

It has been said that the Old Testament is the New Testament concealed, and the New Testament is the Old Testament revealed. The Old Testament contains pictures, or types of spiritual realities more clearly revealed in the New Testament. In addition to the plethora of prophecies regarding the first and second coming of Jesus, many of the stories in the Old Testament foreshadow the life and ministry of Jesus as well.

The story of David and Goliath is clearly one such account. In the Old Testament, the title: *"The Son of David,"* was understood to be a clear reference to the coming Messiah. In a number of Old Testament prophecies, Jesus is called the son of David. For example, the prophet Ezekiel, when speaking of a future day when God would reunite His people, declares:

My servant David will be king over them, and they will all have one shepherd, and they will walk in My ordinances and keep my statutes and observe them.
Ezekiel 37:24

Ezekiel prophesied years after David's death. Yet, God speaks of "David" being king over His people. This King is Jesus. The prophet Isaiah also speaks of Jesus in reference to David and his throne. He writes:

> *For a child will be born to us, a son will be given us; And the government will rest on His shoulders; And His name will be called Wonderful Counselor, Mighty God, Eternal Father, Prince of Peace. There will be no end to the increase of His government or of peace, On the throne of David and over his kingdom, To establish it and to uphold it with justice and righteousness From then on and forever more.*
>
> Isaiah 9:6-7

Many see this portion of Scripture as a prophetic description of Jesus and His coming Kingdom on earth. Sitting on the throne of David, Jesus is the fulfillment of God's promise that *"David shall never lack a man to sit on the throne of the house of Israel"* (Jeremiah 33:17).

Jesus is also called the son of David in the New Testament. He is called this, not because He is the natural born son of David, but because Jesus' "natural" lineage runs through that of David's, thus also qualifying Him to be King. In light of these truths, it should be of no surprise to find some of the events in the life of David as a foreshadowing of Christ and His work.

THE BATTLE OF THE AGES

David's victory over Goliath is a picture of Christ's victory over Satan. The battle between Jesus and Satan is first spoken of in the book of Genesis. After Adam and Eve sinned, God pronounced a curse over both the ground and Satan. Here is a portion of what God said to Satan:

And I will put enmity between you and the woman, and between your offspring and hers; he will crush your head, and you will strike his heel.
Genesis 3:15, NIV

This verse contains what many consider to be the first prophecy about Jesus. Jesus would be "born" of a woman but not conceived in the usual manner. God is His Father. There would be enmity or hostility between Jesus and Satan. God's word clearly states that a battle would take place between them. As a result of this battle, Satan would bruise Jesus' heel, but Jesus would crush Satan's head. The message is that, in this battle, Satan would actually "injure" Jesus, but that Jesus would crush his head. This is an unambiguous reference to the cross and Jesus not only defeating Satan but destroying him!

From this verse from Genesis, it is clear that in the ultimate conflict between Jesus and Satan, there would be a battle. The battle would "take its toll" on both combatants. However, a clear winner would emerge. Jesus would win a decisive victory over Satan.

Let's now look at how David's battle over Goliath foreshadows Christ's victory over Satan. The types and pictures, in my opinion, are undeniable. When we view

David's victory over Goliath alongside Jesus' victory over Satan, we will gain a greater understanding of why, as well as how we can be victorious over our giants.

David is spoken of as the son of Jesse. This places David in the lineage of the promised Messiah. He was also God's choice to be king over Israel. At the time of his battle with Goliath, many were likely unaware of David's anointing to be king. He had not been installed as king at that time. David entered into battle against Goliath with weapons many would consider to be foolish for such a conflict. Yet, David was victorious with them.

As Goliath lied upon the ground, David took his sword. By doing so, he disarmed the giant. Then, David cut off Goliath's head, making a public display of his victory over his enemy. David's victory resulted in victory for Israel as well. His conquest released Israel from potential subservience to their enemy. On the heels of David's victory over Goliath, the army of Israel advanced in victorious battle against the Philistines.

Jesus is described as the son of David. Matthew begins his gospel by saying: *"the book of the generation of Jesus Christ, the son of David"* (Matthew 1:1, NIV). As the son of David, His natural lineage places Him in the lineage of the promised Messiah. Throughout His life and ministry, Jesus battled Satan. In the wilderness, Jesus was tempted. Throughout His ministry, Jesus cast out demons. In response to Jesus healing a dumb and blind man by casting out a demon, the crowd said, *"Is not this the son of David?"* (Matthew 12:23) They believed His authority over demons pointed to Him as being the Messiah of Israel.

As far as His divine lineage is concerned, Jesus is also the only begotten Son of God. Like David, who was the only one willing to confront Goliath, Jesus is the only Son who was able to defeat sin and Satan. As the sinless One, He alone could bear the sins of the world upon the cross and break the powers of darkness.

Regarding His calling to lay down His life upon the cross, Jesus faced temptations designed to discourage Him from doing so. Jesus never gave in to these attempts to keep Him from His purpose. Jesus didn't jump off the pinnacle of the temple and call on angels to rescue Him. He didn't bow to Satan to gain the kingdoms of this world. Jesus didn't allow the people to make Him their earthly king. He didn't listen to Peter when he told him not to give up His life.

Jesus didn't turn from God's will in the Garden of Gethsemane. He didn't call a legion of angels to deliver Him from those who came to take him to the high priest. Jesus didn't defend Himself before Pilate. Simply put, Jesus did not run from the battle. He faced His giant. He battled His enemy, not in a valley, but on a hill called Golgotha, the place of the skull (John 19:17).

Like David, Jesus faced His giant with a "weapon" most would have described as being completely ineffective for the battle He faced. In the eyes of the world, it was foolish for Jesus to have done so. Paul states:

For the message of the cross is foolishness to those who are perishing.
1 Corinthians 1:18, NIV

Nevertheless, Jesus faced Satan, not with a sling, a stone, or a stick but with a wooden cross. There, on the cross, Jesus crushed the serpent's head. He *"disarmed the powers and authorities, he made a public spectacle of them, triumphing over them by the cross"* (Colossians 2:15). Like David, Jesus disarmed Satan and publicly displayed His victory over him. He did so, both during His ministry and by His resurrection from the dead.

As David's victory over Goliath brought victory to the nation, so Christ's victory over Satan makes it possible for us to have victory over our giants as well. Paul speaks of this in his letter to the Romans where he states: *"The God of peace will soon crush Satan under your feet"* (Romans 16:20). Satan bruised Jesus' heal upon the cross, but Jesus crushed His head. Paul tells us that, as a result of our faith in Jesus, **His victory becomes our victory as well.** God will crush Satan under our feet! In his famous hymn, *Hark, the Herald Angels Sing*, Charles Wesley wrote: *"Rise, the woman's conqu'ring seed. Bruise in us the serpent's head."* By grace through faith, we can apply Christ's victory over Satan to our lives, thus giving us victory over our giants! Like David, like Jesus, you can overcome your giant!

Chapter Twelve

YOUR TURN

May I again ask you the question I did when we began:

"David faced a giant named Goliath; what giant are you facing?"

The giant you face is different than the one David faced, but it is every bit as real. It is both fearful and foreboding, and it stands between you and the place God desires to bring you.

Rather than face it, you may have learned to live with it. At times, you even forget that it's there. When you are willing to stay on your side of the valley, it leaves you alone. But as soon as you attempt to break free from your restrictions and move into more of God's plan for your life, it confronts you. Your giant taunts you and discourages you; hurling insults and threats your way, warning you to dare not take even the smallest step forward.

So you freeze. You've learned that you can avoid a battle by remaining where you are, but you know you are not where God has called you. As a result of your hesitancy to fight; you live in fear, failing to experience God's best for your life, content to not engage in a battle that you don't believe you could ever win. It's not the best situation, but it is tolerable, except when you are painfully aware that your giant has enslaved you. You may not be battling your giant, but you are often wrestling with feelings of failure and frustration.

At times you feel hopeful, excited about the possibility of walking in God's best for your life. Then thoughts of your giant in the valley snatches your mind from the dream that awaits you on the next mountaintop. Hope quickly evaporates leaving nothing in its place other than feelings of helplessness. Faith is strangled by fear. Anticipation gives way to anxiety. God is calling you forward. Like Jesus calling out to Peter in the boat, He encourages you to step out and believe He will see you through, but your giant stands in the way. There, in the valley, you find yourself trapped.

You are not alone in your battle. Everyone has either faced a giant, is facing one or will face a giant sometime in their future. That is just how life is. The Bible is full of accounts of individuals who faced opposition, both from without and from within.

We have only looked at one such individual, a young shepherd named David. From his encounter with Goliath, we have seen how David was able to defeat his giant. **David's encounter with Goliath is a picture of the spiritual warfare we all face.** The apostle Paul spoke about this spiritual battle in his letter to the Ephesians. There, he writes, *"For our struggle is not against flesh and blood, but against the rulers, against the powers, against the world forces of this darkness, against the spiritual forces of wickedness in the heavenly places"* (Ephesians. 6:12). The battle we face is every bit as real and as consequential as that which David faced.

But there is good news! Though our giants may appear to be bigger and stronger than us (and they are, that is, in our own strength), God is bigger! Not only is He bigger, He has already defeated them! Hear what the apostle Paul states in his letter to the church at Colossae:

And having disarmed the powers and authorities, he made a public spectacle of them, triumphing over them by the cross.
Colossians 2:15, NIV

Jesus has defeated the enemy that is behind any and every giant we face. He said that all power and authority has been given to Him (Matthew 28:18). While on this earth, every demon was subject to His authority. Through His death, His resurrection and our faith in Him, we have authority over them as well.

The reason why we tend to struggle with giants is because we believe the enemy still has power over us. He does not unless we give him authority over our lives by our decisions. We can give place to the enemy through sin and disobedience. Our choices can lead to our own slavery to giants. It has not been the emphasis of this work to address the ways by which we can empower our giants. I will leave that for others to address. My only instruction to those who seek to be free from the giants they face is to humbly and openly ask God to show you where you may have opened the door for his control to take place in your life. Ask God to reveal to you any areas where your thoughts or actions have allowed giants to enter and remain on the scene. If and when He does, repent and ask God for wisdom how to proceed. Once you have dealt with what you may have done to open a door to the enemy, you can believe God for victory.

Though we can open doors to the enemy, many of the giants we face are the result of the enemy's activities through other people. Satan has a way of lying to us through the things that we have heard and the things we have experienced. He's a master at instilling mindsets and beliefs that are based on lies. He tells a young girl that was molested by a relative that she is dirty and unworthy of love. He tells a boy whom a classmate said was stupid that he will never be able to learn. Years pass, but the giant that entered into their life as a child taunts them at every turn in their adult life.

Again, I ask you: What giant are you facing? What do you believe about yourself that God's Word states not to be true about you? What do you believe about yourself that God doesn't believe about you? Let that question sink in for a moment. What are you called to do that you believe you are incapable of doing? What burden has God placed upon your heart that you have never acted upon because your giant says you aren't qualified to do? What stands in the valley between where you are and where God has called you? If you know you face one, but don't know what it is, then ask God to show you the giant that taunts you and keeps you from moving into all God has for you. God will help you to both identify and defeat the giant you face.

A Proper Mindset

Once you've identified your giant, your freedom is in view. The next step is to see your giant as David saw his. View your giant with a proper mindset, seeing it from a spiritual perspective. David was not concerned with Goliath's physical appearance. He recognized him as a man who was not in covenant relationship with God. Since David was, he knew his spiritual condition was far superior to that of Goliath. David focused on the spiritual reality of the giant he faced.

We must do the same, recognizing that every demonic power is under the authority of Jesus. Since we are in Christ, we have authority over the powers of darkness. There is no demon that can stand against us as we stand in Christ. Demons were subject to Jesus. They were also subject to the disciples. Because of our position in Christ, they are subject to us as well.

Every lie we have been told must bow to the One who is Truth. The source of every lie is the one whom Jesus called the father of lies. As demons must bow to the authority of Jesus, lies must give way to the One who is the Truth. Whatever giant we face, view them with a proper mindset, and you can overcome your giant!

A Powerful Memory

David also had a powerful memory. He recounted before Saul his victories over lions and bears. David snatched sheep from the snare of wild animals, and God protected David from them. David remembered his battles and victories as a shepherd, and his powerful memory of these events gave him the faith to confront Goliath.

As you face your giant, remember all that God has already done in your life. Remember how He saved you out of a life of despair and hopelessness. Remember how God drew you to Himself and brought you into His loving care. As you face your giant, remember the answered prayers, the ways in which God met your needs and the times He brought you through past difficulties. Your memory of God's hand in your life will build your faith to believe that He will help you to overcome your giant.

Proven Methods

In addition to his proper mindset and powerful memory, David had proven methods for battle. With a simple sling and stone, David felled Goliath. David entered into battle with Goliath with that which others would have viewed to be futile against such a foe. Yet David knew these weapons. He knew how to use them. He knew what he could do with them. David chose to fight with the weapons with which he was familiar, and with a simple sling and stone he brought down Goliath.

What are the weapons that God has used in the past to bring you victory? Was it a season of prayer, a promise from His Word that you confessed, a time of fasting? Though the giant you face may be bigger than anything you've wrestled with to this point of your spiritual life, the weapons He has given you for spiritual battle are more than sufficient. It may take a little more prayer, a little more time in the Word or a longer fast (if the Lord leads that way). Nevertheless, you can depend on that which God has shown you, what you have already battled with, to be effective against your giant.

In the eyes of the world, your "weapons" may appear to be quite foolish, even laughable in the face of your giant. Those without spiritual understanding may advise you to simply accept your condition or suggest you rely upon some secular means to cope with your issue. Though there may be some value in counseling, don't settle for living with your giant. Defeat your giant! There are no better weapons for you to do so than those God has given you and that you have tested. The apostle Paul said that, to the world, the cross of Christ was foolishness (1 Corinthians 1:18). Yet, it was through something as "foolish" as His crucifixion and

His resurrection from the dead that the Lord Jesus Christ defeated the powers of darkness.

The weapons of our warfare are not of this world. Paul states:

Though we live in the world, we do not wage war as the world does. The weapons we fight with are not the weapons of the world. On the contrary, they have divine power to demolish strongholds.
2 Corinthians 10:3-4, NIV

They are spiritual in nature and more powerful than anything that any giant can wield against us. As powerful as our weapons may be, our faith does not reside in our weapons, but in our God who has taught us and will teach us how to use them against our giants. Our God never changes. The same God who gave David victory will defeat your giants as well, as you battle with the weapons He has provided and that you have tested through time.

A Propelling Momentum

Goliath taunted David with potentially faith-deflating and discouraging words right up until the battle began. Had David allowed those words to pierce his heart, David's stone might never have penetrated Goliath's head. Just before the battle had been won, David could have given up the fight. How different the story may have ended had David done so.

But he didn't! David responded to Goliath's threats with a declaration of his own. He boldly proclaimed that it would be Goliath, and not him, that would be fed to the birds of the air and the beasts of the field. David countered the words from the giant he faced with a declaration of faith, and it was with these words that David was propelled forward. It was David's words of faith that kept him from running away from his giant. They also provided the propelling momentum to engage and defeat him.

In the midst of a past spiritual battle, do you recall facing a vigorous attack from the enemy, one that hit you just before you were about to have a breakthrough? Have you ever wondered why is it that we struggle the most just before the victory? It is because our giants know when their time is short. They often mount their greatest assault when they sense we are close to overcoming them. The enemy does not know everything, but he is aware of how he can be defeated. It is when we are getting closest to victory that his attacks intensify.

At these moments, just as victory is within reach, we may find ourselves shrinking back. Not only do we cease our fighting at the moment, we may be less willing to engage our giants at a later time. The enemy knows this. He does not want to release us from his grip. He will fight to the finish, for he knows that if we can resist his attempts to discourage us, he will be finished! Therefore, we must recognize that **our giant's intensified attacks are not a sign that they are winning. Rather, it is a sign that we are at the doorstep to victory!**

When you sense fear and discouragement tightening their grip in an effort to strangle your faith, you must speak words of faith. Speak God's Word. Declare what God has promised. Boldly proclaim words of victory, not defeat.

In the face of temptation, Jesus spoke the Word. He confronted the enemy's words with Scripture. When you hear the taunts of your giant, don't let them go unanswered. Respond with words of faith. Remember, God's Word is more powerful that any spoken by any giant we face.

As you speak God's Word, apply your faith to what God has said. By doing so, you will find faith rising in your heart. Your faith in God will provide you with the propelling momentum to confront your giant in battle. Like David, you will overcome your giant.

A Pure Motive

David's greatest weapon against Goliath may well have been his pure motive for victory. David did not seek honor, fame or financial gain, though the king had offered all to the one who would defeat Goliath. David clearly expressed his desire for defeating Goliath, that *"the whole world will know that there is a God in Israel"* (1 Samuel 17:46, NIV). It was God's glory, and not his own, that David desired.

May I ask you this question: "Why do you want to overcome those issues in your life that hold you back?" Are you simply seeking to find personal peace and tranquility? Are you just tired of fighting, tired of struggling and tired of the prolonged battle?

God desires to set you free. He came to heal the brokenhearted, to set the captives free. He does not want you to be enslaved by your giant. He desires for you to walk in full victory and in His perfect plan for your life.

However, **our desire for victory must go beyond personal comfort and liberty. We must desire to reveal God's glory.** If His glory is not our desire, we may fail to realize the reason for, and the purpose of our victory. God desires to set us free because it displays His glory. He is further glorified when we help others experience the freedom we have found in Him.

Like Goliath's sword in David's hand, our testimony of victory over our giant will inspire and build faith in others to believe that they too can overcome their giant. That which the enemy brought against you to destroy you is now a weapon in your hand, a testimony in your mouth that encourages others to overcome the giants they face. Just like the men who were inspired to defeat giants as a result of David's victory over Goliath; your story, for God's glory, will lead to more giants being defeated.

As a further word of encouragement, I'll finish the story about my grade school bully. Remember John, the kid who always picked a fight with me during recess? He was the one who, for days, wrestled me to the ground after lunch. I never fought back for fear that he or his friends would make things worse if I did.

Well, the time came when I had had enough. I finally realized that if something didn't change, then nothing would change. If I continued to allow this kid to bully me without a fight, he would never go away.

On the playground, there was no place for me to flee. Failing to fight back didn't stop the bully's attacks. Reporting what I was experiencing to a teacher may have been the best thing to do, but in my mind, I had only one option left—I had to fight back. I knew it would be risky to do so, but I was tired of being harassed.

When John found me on the playground that day, he came after me as he had each day before. His aggression began like it did every time, but today it would end differently. When he knocked me to the ground, I fought back! Believing that I was taking my own life in my hands, I pushed against him and rolled him onto his back. Then, I placed him in a headlock. At that moment, I sensed that he and his friends would either beat me up or this encounter would finally bring his abuse of me to an end.

As I squeezed with all my might, fearing that releasing him would send me to the nurse's office (or the hospital), John was unable to escape my grasp. I don't know how long I held on to him. It was likely less than a minute, but it seemed like an hour.

When it became obvious to John that he was unable to break free, I let go. With his buddies standing by, John got up and told me that I was lucky that he didn't hurt me. Then he and his friends walked away. That was the last time we ever wrestled!

I do not share this story to encourage fighting, nor do I share it to make you think that it is always a good idea to confront a bully when his friends surround you. I share this story because **there is a time to take a stand against the giant you face**. Had I not stood up to my grade school bully, there's no telling how long he would have continued to torment me.

Have you come to a place in your life that you realize that if something doesn't change, nothing will change? Having read most of this book, are you now aware that there is something that stands between where you are and where God is calling you? If so, I want to encourage you to fight! Face, and battle your giant with a proper mindset, a powerful memory, with proven methods, with propelling momentum and with a pure motive. The same God who helped David defeat Goliath will give you the victory over your giant!

A Fruitful Valley Ahead, But First ...

We began this discussion with two opposing armies on two different mountaintops. Between them was a valley. In this valley stood a giant, demanding his enemies to send out a challenger. The future of both armies and both nations for that matter rested upon the outcome of the confrontation. Losing the battle would result in one nation's slavery to the other, depending on whose warrior was victorious. Avoiding or ignoring the battle would not end the conflict. It would simply keep the army that was unwilling to fight from moving forward. The result of not engaging in battle would be no better than losing. It all came down to a battle in a valley.

At this very moment, you may be facing a similar reality. Your giant is not a nine-foot tall Philistine, and you are not standing on a mountaintop looking into a treacherous valley. However, you know that you are facing a giant. It may be a giant that you may have faced for years. At times, you are able to ignore the giant without it bothering you, that is until you try to move past it. Then, the giant makes his presence known again, freezing you from moving forward. It has mastered you, and you are its servant.

Battling the giant is your only way to victory, but the giant in the valley is frustrating at its best and frightening at its worst. The valley is an intimidating place; it is the place where you come face to face with your giant. Once you enter the battle, there can only be one of two outcomes, you will either be victorious, or your giant will overcome you. Since you are not confident of victory, you fail to fight for fear that you be defeated. The truth is, you are already defeated by your unwillingness to engage your giant.

Life in the Valley

God has a plan for the valleys of your life. He desires to turn your rocky, desert valley into one that is fertile and full of life. He desires to remove the giants that stand in your way and bring you to the next mountaintop. Through God's power, you can overcome your giant. When you do, the valley that was filled with fear and death will become a place of fruitfulness and life.

When you finally overcome your giant, you will be able to look back at your valley and see the fruit that God has brought forth in your life as a result of it. That desolate valley where your giant enslaved you will be turned into a valley flowing with God's blessings. As you share your testimony of God's victory over your giant, you will help others to defeat their giants, thus transforming their valleys as well.

David, a young shepherd, faced a giant named Goliath. David's great God gave him victory over the giant he faced. If you are facing a giant today, know that the same God who gave David victory over Goliath is ready to lead you into victory over your giant. All that is required of you is faith and a willingness to enter into battle. As you do, remember that our "David" has already defeated every giant. On the cross, Jesus overcame all the powers of darkness. Our enemy is defeated. It is time for us to apply His victory. Our giant has been defeated. Move forward in faith, declaring His victory. Through Christ, you can overcome giants!

Your story does not need to end here. Your battle in the valley can lead you to a fruitful valley in the future. Don't settle for where you are. Start taking steps toward victory. Let David's victory over Goliath build your faith for victory in your life as well.

Hopefully, from this book, you've discovered some practical ways to begin to battle and defeat the giant you face. The battle may not be quick or easy, but the results are worth the fight. Does it involve risk? Will you have to take some chances? Yes, but failing to fight may cost you far more.

Never forget: through the cross, Jesus has already defeated any and every giant you face, and you do not have to battle alone. You now have five stones for battle: a proper mindset, a powerful memory, a proven method, a propelling momentum and a pure motive. It's time to move forward!

ABOUT THE AUTHOR

In the mid-1950s, Ron Kramer was born and raised in Milwaukee, Wisconsin. He grew up in a Catholic home but left the church as a teenager. After several years of living away from the Lord, yet searching for truth in his heart, Ron had a life-changing encounter with Jesus Christ midway through his first year of college.

Ron soon became a part of an inter-denominational group of high school and college age believers that first met in a person's home. Later, they gathered weekly in a barn that was converted into a place where meetings could be held. Under the covering of mature believers, this group of young converts experienced New Testament-type fellowship, leadership development, and evangelistic growth.

Ron finished his undergraduate degree in music, but his passion had changed as a result of his conversion. In 1982, Ron attended Christ for the Nations. He graduated in the spring of 1984.

After marrying his wife, Debbie, in February of 1985, Ron worked in the marketplace for 28 years while engaging in lay ministry as a Bible teacher, worship team member and home group leader in non-denominational and Assemblies of God churches in the greater Milwaukee area. He held ministry credentials with the Assemblies of God for about three years. Part of that time, he served as an associate pastor.

In 2012, Ron and his wife felt a call to the Dallas/Fort Worth area where they became involved with Gateway Church. He received his Master's Degree in Practical Theology from the King's University in Southlake, Texas.

After a few years, Ron joined the staff of Gateway Church serving with the adult education department known as Equip. His ministry responsibilities include teaching, developing curriculum and promoting a transformational discipleship experience for those who attend Gateway.

Ron and his wife have been married for over 32 years. Together they had two sons, Jesse and Jordan. Both are now married and serve in full-time ministry. Currently, they have two grandchildren, Molly Rose and Owen Francis.

In addition to his love for teaching, Ron has a passion for writing. Though this is his first published work, he has plans for several more works that include other topics from the life of David as well as a devotional.